VICTORIAN WIVES

Also by Katharine Moore and
published by Allison & Busby

Fiction:
Summer at the Haven
The Lotus House

For children:
The Little Stolen Sweep
Moog

Non-fiction:
She for God: Aspects of Women and Christianity

VICTORIAN WIVES

Katharine Moore

Allison and Busby
LONDON · NEW YORK

This edition first published 1985 by
Allison & Busby Ltd,
6a Noel Street, London W1V 3RB
Distributed in the USA by
Schocken Books Inc,
200 Madison Avenue, New York, NY 10016

First published 1974 by Allison & Busby

British Library Cataloguing in Publication Data

Moore, Katharine
  Victorian wives.
  1. Wives—United States—Biography
  2. Wives—Great Britain— Biography
  I. Title
  920.72'0941   CT3320

  ISBN 0–85031–634–0

Printed and bound in Great Britain by
Richard Clay (The Chaucer Press) Ltd,
Bungay, Suffolk

To the dear memory of my husband
and to H.Fiedler, in whose house
much of this book was written

Contents

"He for God only, she for God in him"
— MILTON, *Paradise Lost*

Introduction

Anthony Trollope has a short passage in *Barchester Towers* which sums up the prevalent Victorian attitude to wives in general and to his own charming heroine, Eleanor Harding, in particular. Eleanor is just about to embark on a second marriage after a respectable period of widowhood. We know that Trollope is writing seriously and not satirically for, in the first place, he is very fond of Eleanor and, in the second, the sentiments he expresses are echoed in most novels, memoirs and poems of the period:

> "When the ivy has found its tower, when the delicate creeper has found its strong wall, we know how the parasite plants grow and prosper . . . Alone they but spread themselves on the ground, and cower unseen in the dingy shade. But when they have found their firm supporter, how wonderful is their beauty."

A very different view of this commonly accepted attitude towards women is given in a bitter fragment of Florence Nightingale's writings:

> "Why have women passion, intellect, moral activity—these three—and a place in Society where no one of these can be exercised? . . . Marriage is but a chance, the only chance offered to women to escape and how eagerly it is embraced."

The pattern of behaviour to which the early and mid-Victorian wife was expected to conform was too often that of a slave among the working classes and in the upper and middle classes of a useless doll. At a period when the working-class woman was subjected to extremes of physical hardship such as no man could be found to endure, ladies, at the price of freedom and intelligence, were pampered and protected to excess:

> "Females from infancy to age are in a state of subjection, nor ought they to consider this a misfortune, on the contrary, it should convince them they are the objects of the fondest solicitude."*

The one form of slavery was in fact dependent on the other.

There were several contributory causes to this state of affairs. Women throughout the centuries had, of course, filled a subordinate position in society and, except for a short period after the Renaissance, had been denied anything like a good all-round education; but before the Industrial Revolution they had at least to become mistresses of household crafts and had been important in their own sphere. As agriculture and cottage industry declined and families flocked to the new town centres, many a country wife had deteriorated into a factory "hand" and the newly prosperous middle class had an unlimited supply of cheap goods and labour so that their wives could live in ignorance and idleness. Indeed it soon became a status symbol that they should do so. The backwash of the late eighteenth-century Romanticism had produced an exaggerated respect for refinement and sensibility, so that the further removed from toil of any kind, the more delicate and empty-headed, the more of a lady was a woman held to be.

The average Victorian middle-class wife in comfortable circumstances was forced to exist in an artificial dependence, sheltered from all reality other than the unavoidable realities of birth and death. Even from the former they were kept as

---

* *The Juvenile Spectator 1810*, a little earlier than our own period, but not out-of-date thirty years later.

much as possible in the dark, although pregnancy and "lying-in", as childbirth was politely termed, became for many of them a more or less perpetual occupation during at least twenty years of their married life. A unique pall of prudery descended on society at this period. Sex for "ladies" was completely taboo, not only any enjoyment, but even any knowledge or recognition of it, and so, because of its undeniable connection with childbirth, any mention of this in public, especially before unmarried girls, or in mixed society, was considered improper. The prudery spread to absurd lengths, yards and yards of upholstery concealed the figure: "a nice girl is very glad of this because if it were not so—just think, people would see one's shape showing! Nice ladies no more thought of showing their legs than did nice chairs."*

Marriage itself in some circles was, as Trollope tells us, "considered almost indelicate to talk about. Engaged young ladies only whisper the news through the very depth of their pink note paper and are supposed to blush as they communicate the tidings by their pens, even in the retirement of their own rooms." As late as 1881 Mrs Ewing, a gifted author, wrote of a friend's wife who was expecting a baby: "Naturally there were many enquiries for Alice arising out of enquiries for you. We got through the *delicate subject* very satisfactorily, considering that a gentleman was present." And Lady Acland, writing of her childhood in the early 'eighties, says: "The truth about how we came to have our being must at all costs—even the cost of deliberate lying—be kept from us. We ate the embryo of fowls for breakfast, but it was devoutly hoped that we did not realise what we were eating."

It was the exception for any "nice" girl to know anything of the facts of life before marriage and very often the ensuing shock put an end once and for all to any hopes of a satisfactory physical relationship between husband and wife, although love, companionship and affection managed often to exist in spite of this. But the following authentic piece of advice on the eve of

* Eleanor Acland, *Goodbye for the Present.*

marriage from a Victorian mother to her daughter was certainly a commonplace of experience, if not of expression, throughout the century: "After your wedding, my dear, unpleasant things are bound to happen, but take no notice of them, I *never* did." A certain Dr Acton pronounced that any attribution of sexual pleasure to women was a "vile aspersion". The average husband not only took this ignorance for granted but desired it, as in his mind ignorance was equated with innocence:

> Pure as a bride's blush
> When she says "I will" unto she knows not what.
> [Coventry Patmore]

Often the first pregnancy was as much of a mystery and horror as the wedding night and the young wife supposed herself to be seriously ill. My own grandmother remained ignorant of what was happening to her until her first child was well on the way. When enlightened by an observant friend, she was incredulous. Third in a family of eight, she had been successfully kept completely in the dark as to how her five younger brothers and sisters had arrived. Even when recognised, the expectant mother's state had to be hushed up and concealed as far as possible and the voluminous skirts and petticoats seemed specially designed for this. When the baby arrived it was the fashion to hand it over to a wet-nurse and later a whole army of cheap female labour in the shape of nurses, under-nurses and governesses took over. Lady Cecilia Ridley, an enlightened and affectionate mother, wrote about her small son: "I find him a very agreeable companion and I like taking him out to walk whenever possible without any of my odious nurses." Boys graduated in time to tutors and boarding schools and there were also aunts and elder sisters at hand till it was rare for a well-to-do mother to see her own children for more than a short period each day.

The actual size of the family and the strain of constant pregnancies added to the artificially created barriers.* Of course a woman with strong maternal feelings, reasonable health and resolution managed to a certain extent to break away from this pattern of helplessness and estrangement and took an active part in organising her nursery and schoolroom. But one has only to look at the novels of the period to see that such mothers were the exception. Florence Nightingale continues her passionate outburst thus: "A woman cannot live in the light of intellect. Society forbids it. Those conventional frivolities which are called 'her duties' forbid it. The Family uses people, not for what they are but for what it wants them for . . . this system dooms some minds to incurable infancy, others to silent misery." The family, or in other words, the Victorian idea of the family, was that the wife and mother should be a delicate clinging parasite and undoubtedly the child-wife was often the result. "Ha! poor Baby!" said Miss Trotwood to Mrs Copperfield on the eve of David's birth. "Do you know *anything?*" The answer was too obviously "no"—and Dora Copperfield, the prototype of all such pathetic victims to the prevailing fashion, exclaims when David tries to explain to her that he must now earn his living:

> " 'Don't talk about being poor and working hard—oh don't, don't!'
> " 'My dearest love,' said I, 'the crust well earned—'
> " 'Oh, yes, but I don't want to hear any more about crusts!' said Dora, 'and Jip [her pug] must have his mutton chop every day at twelve, or he'll die.' "

Unfortunately this sort of thing was what the Victorian husband was conditioned to accept. David was charmed with Dora's childish winning ways: "I fondly explained to her that

---

* We need not be smug about this. Our own age has replaced these problems by its own: the broken home, the commuting mother and the skyscraper flat.

Jip should have his mutton chop every day." And although the disadvantages were obvious, the concept of the helpless innocent child-wife was flattering, and therefore cherished by the Victorian patriarchal society, while the clever enquiring minds, the passionate dominant natures, were, as Florence Nightingale said, too often condemned to silent misery or were ridiculed and shunned. Even the lucky ones, who with the aid of sympathetic fathers, brothers and husbands, managed to break through the prevailing image, to educate themselves in odd moments and to find some charitable work to do, were faced with formidable difficulties. The husband was so much more the dominant figure in the family and in society: "She for God in him" was so much the accepted maxim, that for a wife to develop her own personality was uphill work. How could it be otherwise when the ideal wife is made to exclaim in one of the most popular poems of the day, Coventry Patmore's *The Angel in the House* :

> From that time [her marriage] many a Scripture text
> Helped me, which had before perplexed.
> Oh, what a wondrous world seems this,
> He is my head, as Christ is his!
> None ever could have dared to see
> In marriage such a dignity
> For man, and for his wife no less
> Such happy, happy lowliness.

Another influential book, Ruskin's *Sesame and Lilies* (1865), contains a section written specially for middle-class women—"Lilies: of Queen's Gardens". It is interesting how often lilies, the symbols of purity and of virginity, appear in the literature and painting of the period. Ruskin disposes of the "rights" of women (his own quotation marks) in his characteristic summary fashion: "Of all the insolent, all the foolish persuasions that by any chance could enter and hold your empty little heart." The theme of the book is the separate spheres allotted by God to the two sexes—the woman's turning out to be none other than the old one of wifely duty. She is allowed her throne "where men may bow before the myrtle crown and the stainless sceptre of womanhood" but it soon appears that in return for this and for being "protected from all danger and temptation" she must in all things hold herself in subjection to her King. As for education, that must be directed first and foremost "to their true constant duty", hence "a man ought to know any language or science he learns thoroughly; while a woman ought to know the same language and science only so far as may enable her to sympathise in her husband's pleasure, and in those of his best friends". A woman must "grow effortlessly like flowers". She must practise piety but not bother with theology. She must be noble and never frivolous. Ruskin does allow his Queens to exercise a strictly rationed benevolence but it must never interfere with her sacred duty as a wife: "If the hostile society of the outer world is allowed to cross the threshold [of the house] it ceases to be a home [but] wherever a true wife comes, this home is always round her. The stars only may be over her head, the glow-worm in the night-cold grass may be the only fire at her feet, but home is wherever she is and for a noble woman it stretches far round her, better than ceiled with cedar or painted with vermilion." It is questionable how far the many wretched working Victorian wives found the practice of noble home-making compatible with conditions which often were as cold and as unprotected, though not so poetical, as those which Ruskin describes. However he was of course addressing himself to the middle-class wife, the dedicated, pure and obedient Queen of the Englishman's castle.

Tennyson's *The Princess* makes a blundering attempt at sympathy with the rebellious Florence Nightingales but the impact is dulled by the poet giving this tale of a women's college community a medieval setting; "the Splendour falls on Castle Walls" and, in such a romantic golden light, it is safe to play with so revolutionary a theme. Besides, it all ends well. Princess Ida's brave venture is overcome and her bid for independence conquered by the fainting Prince appealing to her laudable maternal instincts and, though lip service is paid to "a dream" of equality in the dim future, the poem finishes with the hero's injunction to Ida to "lay thy sweet hands in mine and trust to me". Marriage after all is shown to be the only true fulfilment for women.

There are plenty of lilies in *The Princess* and pure white robes floating round; Ida's followers are likened to "a troop of snowy does" and the young girl, whose longing to go to college "like a man" sets the whole poem going, is called Lilias. Her wild talk is received with laughing indulgence for "her petulance" and she is described as "a rosebud set with little wilful thorns". (A rose, by the way, is not so meritorious as a lily in the Victorian language of flowers and in fact by the end of the century it has developed a questionable association with another less desirable aspect of womanhood.) However, Lilias profits by the tale of Princess Ida and so no doubt did many a contemporary. For Coventry Patmore, Ruskin and Tennyson were only the most golden-tongued among the multitude of those who felt that for wives to aim at anything like mental equality with their husbands was out of the question. Even Rousseau, the liberator, had written: "The whole education of women ought to be relative to men. To please them, to be useful to them, to make themselves loved and honoured by them, to educate them when young, to care for them when grown . . . these are the duties of women at all times, and what should be taught them from infancy."

John Stuart Mill's *The Subjection of Women* (1869) was a voice in the wilderness, and the "immorality" of this book was everywhere condemned. One reviewer wondered how "this madman" could conceive that the relation between the sexes might ever "work on a purely voluntary principle" and thirty years after its publication it was still considered wickedly anarchistic. This immoral writer believed that justice towards women should replace chivalry. Mill realised that great educational and judicial reforms were necessary to make justice possible, especially for the wife and mother. In the eyes of the law, when Mill published his book, the married woman was classed with lunatics, criminals and minors. Blackstone's commentary on the marriage law stated that "the very being or legal existence of the woman is suspended during marriage".

At the beginning of the Victorian period a mother had no rights whatever over her children, however vicious or irresponsible their father might be. The courageous and passionate fight made by Caroline Norton to regain her children resulted in the Custody of Infants Bill of 1839 whereby a mother was allowed rights over children up to seven years old but no further concessions were made in this direction during the rest of our period.* A wife could not obtain divorce until 1857 and then it was based on a double-standard premiss and granted only for desertion and cruelty and not for adultery. It was, besides, so expensive as to be absolutely prohibitive to almost any woman, for a wife had no legal right to any property, not even any wages she might earn by her own exertions. Charlotte Brontë could pocket her own royalties from the sales of *Jane Eyre*, but Mrs Gaskell had to, and did, hand over every penny she received from *Cranford* and the rest of her novels to her husband. The Married Woman's Property Act was not passed till 1870. When the bill first had come up for discussion fifteen years earlier, the *Saturday Review* had remarked that "for married women to make wills set at defiance the commonsense of mankind", and even after the act had been passed, Lord Fraser voiced the general attitude of husbands: wives were "already sufficiently protected and why they should be allowed to have money in their pockets to deal with as they think fit I cannot understand." Their complete financial dependence resulted in lack of responsibility. It encouraged the doll mentality (we have seen how poor Dora Copperfield reacted to David's difficulties), and together with the purposelessness of their lives produced in

* One hundred and thirty years later the British Government has issued a report recommending that both parents should be given equal rights over their children.

many women a distressingly negative frame of mind.

Punch, often a reliable indication of contemporary thought, ridicules, patronises and admonishes women by turns. In an 1870 issue a serious paragraph entitled "Women's Worst Disabilities" appeared in which *Punch* remarks: "Women in general (not you, sweet readers) are in the habit . . . of saying non possemus, 'I can't take exercise', 'I can't dress under so much a year', 'I can't do without a carriage', 'I can't manage without so many servants', 'I can't do anything whatever that implies the least degree of self-command.' " The Married Woman's Property Act was not fully amended so as to be effective until 1908, so that throughout the whole of our period the Victorian wife was legally economically entirely at the mercy of her Lord and Master.

It is interesting to compare the position of nineteenth-century wives with those across the Atlantic, where men and women stemming from the same traditions, and subject to the same common law, were working out their relationship rather differently. There was never quite the same degrading pattern in the States. Women there, as over here, had "many duties but few rights" but whereas English Victorian custom confirmed and increased the dependence of the middle-class wife, dissimilar forces were at first active in the New World. The Southern States differed again but these were too far removed from English society to provide a useful comparison.

In the first place, where there was a shortage of all kinds of labour, women were found to be indispensable. The first settlers' wives were more akin to the medieval housewife, the mistress of many crafts. She had to weave and spin and provide many of the different necessities of a primitive community, as well as to carry out her ordinary household skills. She was therefore of great importance. Then, during the late eighteenth and nineteenth centuries there were frontier wars and national wars, as well as the dangers of a pioneering life, to face. In all times of such stress, when the men have had to leave home, women have come into their own (we have seen it happening in the last two great wars of the twentieth century). During these unsettled times wives had to manage their husbands' estates, businesses and farms, and they shared all the hazards of the frontier pioneer states. It was of no use to prate of refinement, propriety or delicacy, nor of the bloom of innocence when there were wounded men to be nursed and hungry mouths to feed and a man's work to be carried on somehow. In such conditions, in spite of the law and the prophets, men and women grew inescapably to view each other as equal partners in the job of living. The War of Independence had widened the gulf between the old world and the new and gave women the opportunity which they seized upon for organising themselves for the first time in history in the successful effort to supply clothes for the troops. This was one hundred years before any comparable self-organising activity in England. So, at the Declaration of Independence it did occur to one wife, Abigail Edwards, to write to her husband: "In the new code of laws which I suppose it will be necessary to make, I desire you will remember the ladies." The phrase "natural and inalienable rights" seemed as though it ought to apply to both sexes.

During the Civil War women served in thousands, as nurses, and some even as spies and soldiers, and this made them feel that they had a just claim on the State. In 1870, when the vote was granted "to all citizens without regard to colour", women asked: "Are we not citizens too?" Actually in the Pioneer West in Wyoming, women were allowed to vote as early as 1869 and by 1896 three more Western States had women's suffrage and some few others adopted a limited suffrage. English women had to wait till 1918 for their own limited suffrage. It is perhaps worth noting that at the first joint poll in Wyoming a Quaker grandmother was the first to march into the polling booth and that as a result of the women's vote there was less roughness, shooting and drinking at the elections. When, in 1890, Wyoming was made a State and Washington tried to get it to repudiate the women's vote, the reply was that Wyoming would rather stay out of the Union a hundred years than do so, and this carried the day.

The anti-slavery campaign also brought American women to the fore. Their sympathy for the slaves was that of one second-class citizen for another. They wrote and organised with untiring energy. The campaign also developed women as lecturers and public speakers. Quakers were active in the New World, and amongst Quakers women have always been encouraged to share equally with men both in speaking and in the business concerns of the Society, so it is not surprising to find that it was a Quaker, Prudence Crandall, who in 1833 first set the example to women in public speaking. As late as 1870 in England, however, such a phenomenon as a lady addressing a public meeting was treated as a disgrace.

Again, as early as 1781, ten years before Mary Wollstone-craft published her famous but almost unheeded *Vindication of the Rights of Women*, an American wife, Judith Sargent Murray, had written: "Is it reasonable that a candidate for immortality, for the joys of heaven, an intelligent being, should at present be so degraded as to be allowed no other ideas than those which are suggested by the mechanism of a pudding or the sewing of the seams of a garment?" English society at that time and for long after had decided that it *was* reasonable, but Mrs Murray a few years later was able triumphantly to exclaim: "Female Academies are everywhere established and right pleasant is the appellation to my ear." One of these, early in the nineteenth century, was started by Catherine Beecher, the sister of Harriet Beecher Stowe, author of *Uncle Tom's Cabin*, and to it Harriet herself came and learned enough Latin between her twelfth and thirteenth years to translate Ovid into rhymed verse. Again this was about thirty years before Charlotte Yonge's Ethel May of *The Daisy Chain* was striving to teach herself a little Latin with the aid, when she could get them, of her father's spectacles and her brother's schoolbooks. This same Catherine Beecher horrified a German professor by writing a successful theological argumentative pamphlet: "You have a woman that can write thus? God forgive Christopher Columbus for discovering America."

Women feminists in the New World were more extreme in their views than their corresponding numbers in England. There was a group led by Elizabeth Stanton and Susan Anthony who attacked the institution of marriage itself. One of Mrs Stanton's friends wrote: "Woman's chief discontent is not with her political, but with her social, and particularly her marital, bondage." Lucy Stone in 1855 made the occasion of her marriage an opportunity for protest. The clergyman officiating declared: "I never performed the marriage ceremony without a renewed sense of the inequity of our present system of laws in respect to marriage; a system by which 'man and wife are one, and that one is the husband'. It was with my hearty concurrence, therefore that the following protest was read and signed as part of the nuptial cenermony." The protest was against the sole property rights of the husband and asserted a belief in personal independence and equal human rights and in an equal and permanent partnership.

Easier divorce was advocated by some women and this was adopted in certain States. Mrs Osborne, an American, in order to marry Robert Louis Stevenson, had to return to California to get her divorce, which it was impossible for her to obtain in England. She was unprepared for the hostility and suspicion that she met with in English society on account of this divorce. It is interesting, in passing, to note that Stevenson met her in the Artists' Colony at Grez, near Paris, where she was the first woman to invade the hitherto exclusive male community.

The comparatively enlightened state of women in the New World was reflected in small but not unimportant ways. Married women and even girls were free to go about alone and to ride in public conveyances on their own. This was unheard of for ladies in England. As regards young ladies, says Trollope: "it is generally understood that there are raging lions about the metropolis . . . In New York and Washington there are supposed to be no lions." In a pleasantly amusing little book

The American Girl in London published as late as 1891, the heroine answers the anxious enquiries of an English friend as to a suitable companion for her travels: "I can go round London beautifully by myself." "By yourself!" exclaimed her English friend, "this is an independent young American indeed! But you'll have to get over *that* idea. Your friends will never in the world allow it, and do I understand that your parents of their own free will permitted you to cross the Atlantic alone?"

The American girl also comments on the attitude of English husbands to their wives' clothes:

> " 'I will *not* have you in stripes!' I heard him say as I passed, full of commiseration for her. What arrogance! I thought, 'In America they are glad to have us in anything.'
>
> "It struck me that we had never been thankful enough that our husbands and fathers are too much occupied to make purchases for their families."

On the question of rational clothes, American women were again in the forefront for though the invention of the bloomer in the mid-century proved abortive, it none the less had its effect. The baggy Turkish trousers to hide the provocative and therefore forbidden leg, and the full short skirt and uncorseted waist provided a wonderful escape from cumbersome and unhealthy fashions and freedom and ease of movement for the busy housewife. Mrs Amelia Bloomer, though not the inventor, was the prettiest of the daring wives who adopted this costume and so lent her name to it—but, alas, public feeling against it proved too strong. Prudery was certainly as rife in the New World as the Old, but the women there wore it with a difference. It was carried to such ridiculous outward lengths as almost to defeat its own ends. Mrs Trollope, with her sharp critical observation, felt it to be so affected in mixed company as to be almost like a charade and remarked that, when by themselves, the wives and girls were far from prudish. The ignorance which was strictly and successfully imposed upon their English cousins seemed, with them, to be assumed. The preoccupation of the American husband with his own affairs, commented on favourably by the American girl in London, and the marked difference in behaviour in mixed and single-sex gatherings noticed by Mrs Trollope, was associated with the American habit of dining apart. This struck Mrs Trollope as very strange and unpleasant. It certainly resulted in inferior table manners and it had other more important disadvantages, yet may it not also have encouraged greater freedom and independence in American wives?

However this may be, it is certainly a fact that from pioneering days onwards, a number of factors contributed to a more emancipated conception of women's place in society in America, at least during the greater part of the Victorian era. Later, partly through the influence of Freud, there seems to have been something of a reaction. Freud, like Rousseau, confined his revolutionary ideas to men only. On the subject of women he was reactionary. He was a great advocate of separate spheres—women's role is the passive one and their only duty to be wives and mothers. In his attitude to his fiancée he is typically Victorian: "My sweet child—my gentle sweet girl. I implore you to withdraw from the struggle into the calm uncompetitive activity of my home."

The United States took readily to the new psychology and its effect was felt in the Women's Movement, but the strength of the earlier revolutionary period was still active and it is significant that the Women's Liberation Movement of today began in the New World and reveals there its most militant aspect.

This introduction has aimed at giving an idea of the social attitudes towards women and marriage which were common in the Victorian era. Against this background I have traced, in the following chapters, the lives of some individual Victorian wives. These are not arranged in strict chronological order. I have begun with Mrs Coventry Patmore as she seemed the most representative of the popular image, and have ended with Mrs George MacDonald, whose marriage came nearest to a breakaway from the conventional pattern. The three American wives included each achieved a degree of independence, illustrative of the greater freedom allowed to New Englishwomen.

It is, of course, only rather exceptional individuals, outstanding either for special gifts or personality, or because of unusual circumstances, who have left any public records of their lives. For examples of the more typical Victorian wife we must turn to fiction. In the great novelists of the period we find plenty of descriptions of the married lives of such women and of what their creators thought about them. In art it is always more possible to see a definite pattern and the chronological development of ideas between, for instance, Dickens and Meredith, George Eliot and Henry James, is not difficult to follow. In romantic poetry too the lilies and angels of the early Tennyson and Patmore give place, as the century wanes, to the "roses and raptures" of Swinburne and Rossetti. The erring woman becomes not so much an object of horror as of fascination, and this attitude again changes to one of sombre compassion in the poems and prose of Thomas Hardy.

"He for God only, she for God in him"—this Miltonic maxim upon the relative attitudes appropriate in marriage would have been accepted without question in almost every household in nineteenth-century England. It did not work too well in Milton's Eden, neither did it in the Victorian home.

I

The Angel in the House

The Three Mrs Coventry Patmores
1824-1862

Emily Andrews, the first Mrs Coventry Patmore, was to a greater extent than Jane Morris or Elizabeth Siddall the pre-Raphaelite ideal. She looked the part so thoroughly that she was a favourite subject for painters and sculptors, though none caught the essence of the image so well as Browning in his poem "The Face" for which Emily was the inspiration :

> If one could have that little head of hers
> Painted upon a background of pale gold,
> Such as the Tuscan's early art prefers!
> No shade encroaching on the matchless mould
> Of those two lips, that should be opening soft
> In the pure profile—not as when she laughs,
> For that spoils all—but rather as aloft
> Some hyacinth she loves so leaned its staff's
> Burthen of honey coloured studs to kiss
> Or capture, twixt the lips, apart for this.
> Then her little neck, three fingers might surround,
> How it should waver on the pale gold ground
> Up to the fruit-shaped perfect chin it lifts.

Here, certain key words and phrases—"little", "Tuscan art", "soft", "pure", "not as when she laughs", "pale gold ground"

—leave a clear impression on our minds of a sacred yet sensuous beauty, serious but inviting, always virginal, even though the honey should be sipped and the fruit plucked. She was never to escape from her destiny as the "angel in the house". Indeed, it was not only in looks that Emily fulfilled the ideal. She really was angelic: unselfish, sweet-tempered, devoted, intelligent. Too soon she also showed herself typical of the Victorian heroine in other and less desirable ways. She was delicate, worn out by child-bearing and died young—her deathbed was prolonged and poetic, or at least provided matter for poetry.

Coventry Patmore, with his mystic eroticism, his yearning for both purity and passion, was unique amongst his contemporaries, not for this, but for his determination to experience it without diminution within the sanctity of marriage and in his desire and capacity to embody the experience in poetry. Emily was in every particular just what the age and her husband demanded, the "angel in the house", and she was so to the end of her short life without self-pity or rebellion or reproach or any hint of ugliness or failure. She had not much sense of humour perhaps, but this was not required of her—indeed, rather the reverse. But at the beginning it was May among the fields and lanes of Hampstead, where Keats had listened to his nightingale, and where the hawthorn and apple blossom matched in sweetness,

> in flushed array
> Of white and ruddy flower, auroral gay,

the demeanor of "the destined maid" whom her lover meets "by heavenly chance".

She was an orphan, twenty-three years old, poor but well educated, and he was twenty-four, handsome and a poet whose verses she had read. He had a small assured income as Assistant Librarian at the British Museum, there seemed no reason to wait, so they were married before the summer was out, and

4

Patmore lost no time in getting to work on his great poem which was to extol the glory of marriage.

Luckily Emily was a practical "angel" (indeed she published a manual called *The Servants Behaviour Book*) for there was not much money and children came quickly. If they had been characters in one of Trollope's novels he would never have allowed them to marry on such an insufficient income. But in spite of all her duties and cares she did not lose her charm. We have glimpses of her from sources other than her husband's poetry; Ruskin, Carlyle, Tennyson, Millais and Holman Hunt all admired her. Millais's portrait shows her with "great brown eyes under the heavy curtain of voluminous dark hair . . . the complexion is transparently hectic . . . the whole candid face and high-poised head breathes an indomitable earnestness and purity. One feels that this finely-coloured creature will be living all for duty and the ideal." (This seems to have been true and not only of Emily but of other Victorian matrons. How did they manage it and at what cost?) No wonder Coventry Patmore declared at this time that Millais's work showed far greater genius than Keats's.

Another contemporary wrote of Emily that she combined "a strange beauty with extreme innocence of manner". This again was the current ideal and Patmore, for his part, strove "to mortify the lusts of the flesh" and prayed that his conscience might become healthier and more proportionate, a prayer the more significant when we remember that after his death a complete set of reprints of the world's erotic literature was found hidden in his library. Emily responded, as he recorded, with absolute devotion and understanding, "feeling every vibration of my irregular moods, yet never showing impatience." He saw her always in relation to himself.

Angels, of course, do not have moods nor lusts of the flesh and, indeed, poor Emily had not much time nor energy for either. Six children followed each other in quick succession, the household had to be run on the same small income and the babies kept quiet while their father worked on his great poem.

There were frequent moves, sometimes to furnished lodgings so that money could be saved, and Emily willingly sacrificed her own comfort and health so that he could work in peace. Patmore does seem to have been conscious of this sacrifice to a certain extent. He admired the books for children she managed to produce: "You ought really to do something . . . now all your light will be swallowed up in mine." But that this should be so was so inevitable, so thoroughly accepted by both that it is hardly a regret.

In 1854 the first part of *The Angel in the House* appeared. Ruskin characteristically praised it as "blessedly popular *doing good* wherever it goes!" Tennyson called it "one of the very small number of great poems in the world". Emerson made it known and loved in the States "and recited by young and old, an ever enlarging company". Nathaniel Hawthorn told Patmore "that I thought his popularity would be greater in America—we had a general gift of quicker and more subtle recognition of genius . . . It is a poem for happy married people to read together . . . but I doubt whether the generality of English people are capable of appreciating it." This doubt however proved unfounded for its popularity was only rivalled by Tennyson's *Idylls of the King*. The exchange of compliments between these two poets on their respective "angels" (both called Emily) is enlightening in its emphasis on certain qualities. Tennyson speaks enthusiastically of Emily Patmore's "innocence and simplicity" and Patmore describes Emily Tennyson to his wife as having "that high cultivation which is found only in the upper classes. She is neither brilliant or literary at all. She seems to understand Tennyson thoroughly and waits upon him and attends to him as she ought to do." The poem has, of course, completely gone out of fashion and Patmore is chiefly praised now for his later work but it has great social interest and some charm. It also is unique in its subject which is the mystical significance of married love. It was no secret that Emily was the inspiration for the "angel" and this gave the poem a special significance. But the angel was also the soul, and the house the body, and the relation between wife and husband was, on a deeper level, symbolic of that between the soul and God.

It is a curious work to study today; a madly incongruous mixture of Donne and Trollope, for Donne, too, celebrates love between husband and wife and Patmore sometimes echoes his music, yet with the significant difference that whereas Donne emphasises equality and union which is the essence of love, Patmore underlines that sense of "otherness" and distance between the sexes, which is the essence of romance.

> He who would seek to make her his
> Will comprehend that souls of grace
> Own sweet repulsion, and that 'tis
> The quality of their embrace
> To be like the majestic reach
> Of coupled suns, that, from afar,
> Mingle their mutual spheres, while each
> Circles the twin obsequious star.

The Trollopian background to this sort of mystical treatment is a series of thoroughly Victorian scenes—afternoon tea on the lawn, hunt balls, the carriage and pair of bays, Aunt Maud and the Dean, a picnic, gloves, violets—"Papa had bid her send his love and would he dine with us next day"—at its best full of a nostalgic charm.

> Red-brick and ashlar, long and low,
> With dormers and with oriels lit.
> Geranium, lychnis, rose array'd,
> The windows, all wide open thrown;
> And some one in the Study play'd
> The Wedding March of Mendelssohn.

And at its worst, scattered at any moment throughout, lines of astonishing bathos, as these, the final end to a poem of high mystical intent :

7

> But here, their converse had its end
> For crossing the Cathedral lawn
> There came an ancient college friend,
> Who, introduced to Mrs Vaughan,
> Lifted his hat, and bow'd and smiled,
> And filled her kind large eyes with joy
> By patting on the cheek, her child
> With "Is he yours, this handsome boy?"

These lapses could be due to Patmore's lack of humour and of any self-criticism, but what of his manifold admirers including most of the great ones of the period? The mid-Victorian sense of congruity, humour, call it what you will, obviously differed enormously from ours. Possibly light may be thrown on this by Meredith's observation that the appreciation of true comedy can only flourish in a society in which men and women share some common ground and at least approximate to equality. Now, the qualities in women most praised by Coventry Patmore are those which emphasise difference and inequality between the sexes. First in importance comes the purity which is based upon ignorance—

> Pure as a bride's blush when she says
> I will, unto she knows not what.

This virginal quality, however, is to survive marriage and on her part the ideal seems to be a sort of immaculate conception, for

> Why having won her do I woo
> Because her spirit's *vestal* grace
> Provokes me always to pursue
> But spirit-like, eludes embrace.
>
> That splendid brow of chastity
> That soft and yet subdueing light

8

shines forth undimmed and

> Reflects a light of hopeless snows
> That bright in *virgin* ether bask.

In spite of his embraces,

> This Temple keeps its shrine
> Sacred to Heaven.

Closely related to purity is the quality of modesty :

> Her modesty, her cheerful grace
> The cestus clasping Venus side
> How potent to deject the face
> Of him who would affront its pride
>
> Know she, who in her dress reveals
> A fine and modest taste, displays
> More loveliness than she conceals.

Honor (alias Emily), the perfectly modest wife, when she is asked for her comments on "the fumes of early love my verse has figured" replies :

> You speak too boldly, veils are due
> To women's feelings . . .
> I did not call you "Dear" or "Love"
> I think till after Frank was born.

But possibly gentleness is even more in demand than purity, for even a prostitute may be forgiven if she

> With a woman's error still
> Preserve a woman's gentleness.

And

> A woman's gentle mood o'er stept
> Withers my love.

The word "gentle", or "gentleness", occurs on almost every page; naturally Honor "is compact of gentleness". It is used to describe her interchangeably with "sweet", "womanly" and "pure"; "She was fulfilled in gentleness".

> In every look, word, deed and thought
> Nothing but sweet and womanly
> She is so lovely, pure and true . . .
> You paint, Miss Churchill ?—pray go on.

This being, so removed from man in her virginal, modest gentleness, must also differ from him in capacity and aims. She must

> want the will of men
> To conquer fame . . .

She must also

> want the patient brain
> To track shy truth.

Instead she is allowed facility, intuition, and encouraged to retain childlikeness and simplicity :

> She grows
> More infantine, auroral, mild
> And still the more she lives and knows
> The lovelier she's expressed a child

and "Around her mouth a baby smile" is held to be an enchantment. It is inevitable then that though the purer spirit, this simple, childlike, gentle creature must look up to and defer to her husband in all earthly affairs:

> Her strength is your esteem, beware
> Of finding fault; her will's unnerved
> By blame; from you t'would be despair
> But praise that is not quite deserved
> Will all her noble nature move.

But something further is expected—a total abnegation once marriage vows have been exchanged:

> Man must be pleased: but him to please
> Is woman's pleasure, down the gulf
> Of his condoled necessities
> She casts her best.

If he prove unworthy the situation as far as she is concerned remains unchanged:

> And if he once by shame oppress'd
> A comfortable word confess
> She leans and weeps against his breast
> And seems to think the sin was hers.

This image of the perfect wife, pure, inviolable, unintellectual, gentle, self-sacrificing, utterly devoted, is not Patmore's invention, though he found it greatly to his taste. It is present in most of the famous novels of the day (yet conspicuously absent from the works of the great women writers: the Brontë sisters, Mrs Gaskell and George Eliot). Its angelic wings hover uneasily over Thackeray's pages, it presides at the hearths and homes and deathbeds of Charles Dickens, and, curiously, it holds determined sway among the singularly strong minds of Trollope's heroines. But Patmore's is the most concentrated and exalted presentation of this ideal.

It is easy in viewing the poem primarily as a period piece to do less than justice to its finer passages, yet even these are tainted with this peculiarly vitiating mid-Victorian concept of the proper relation between the sexes, and many a Victorian wife may have suffered, though for the most part unconsciously, from the immense popularity of *The Angel in the House*.

The last volume of the poem was published after Emily's death. She had caught the fatal cold which developed into consumption as early at 1857 and by 1861 there was no hope of recovery. The Victorians, so full of repressions over sex, had none over death. We have reversed this; what would we think now of a young mother who went to choose the site of her own grave? Or of a young father who wrote to his schoolboy son: "Remember that you are not likely to have your poor Mama long so you should make the best of the time you have left to please her . . . Although your learning well is very important, there are other things much more important . . . to be *pure* (you know what I mean). If you are not pure . . . you will not see your dear Mama any more when she is once gone."

Emily had time to think of everything and she shows both her unselfishness and her perception in her last preoccupations; she was anxious over the children's future relations with their father, for she had always been the mediator between his moods, his impatience and his demands, and their growing need for understanding and liberty. She too, like Emily Tennyson, thoroughly comprehended her husband. She knew he could not live without a wife, and to the second "angel" she left her wedding ring with her love and blessing. She was deeply troubled lest he should become a Catholic, having like so many devout English people at that time a horror of such a step: "When I am gone—the priests will get you and then I shall see you no more." Coventry disclaimed this earnestly yet this is just what he did only three years later.

After her death Patmore wrote one of his most famous

poems "Departure". It is a beautiful poem in some ways and in judging it one must remember the Victorian attitude towards death, so alien to us: the exploitation of grief which it often seems to express. Yet, granted all this, there is something which grates on the heart in the self-regarding tone of certain lines:

> But all at once to leave me at the last
> And go your journey of all days
> With not one kiss or a goodbye
> And the only loveless look, the look with which you
>   passed.

More distasteful is the fact that he cared about the praise such a poem brought him from the public. Even though it was years later it is unpleasant to read a letter to Gosse referring to a review of his collected poems: "When I came to the Departure I ended by purring and assured myself that although readers of the Saturday would look upon DV and Widow Neale as my average, still they would see that in one or two happy moments I could rise above it."

The well-known poem "The Toys" also has a touching appeal but one cannot help feeling that Patmore himself is a little too conscious of its poignancy. It tells of the stern treatment of his little motherless son and of how, later, he finds him asleep with tears on his cheeks and all his toys arranged around him for comfort:

> My little son, who look'd from thoughtful eyes
> And moved and spoke in quiet grown-up wise,
> Having my law the seventh time disobey'd
> I struck him and dismissed
> With hard words and unkissed,
> His mother, who was patient, being dead.

Patmore told a friend that the poem referred to his eldest son,

Milnes, and this certainly fits in with the boy's reputation as a rebel and with his relationship with his father; but as he was past fourteen and a naval cadet at the time of his mother's death, it looks as if the line, "His mother, who was patient, being dead", was added for effect, as the incident must have occurred earlier when Milnes was a small child. However that may be, the alternate harshness and self-reproach expressed in the poem were authentic in Patmore's relation to his children. Whatever he had been as a husband, he was not an ideal father and Emily knew this, when she hoped for a second marriage for him. Milnes and he were increasingly alienated from the time of her death. "You have forgotten the vows made beside your mother's coffin", he wrote when he received unsatisfactory reports of the boy. It has been suggested that his attitude towards his children was influenced by a well-founded conviction that frequent child-bearing had weakened Emily's resistance to consumption.

None the less Patmore did try at times to be a good father and showed touches of insight and real affection, especially to his daughters. Like so many Victorian men, including Ruskin, Lewis Carroll and Burne Jones, Patmore had a decided weakness for little girls. With his eldest daughter he had always had a special relationship. When she was a baby he wrote: "Such eyes! She shall never marry with my consent if she looks so handsome!" She was from the first a rare creature, but she was still only a child when he discovered Marianne Boyles, "the beauty of whose personality seemed to be the pure effulgence of Catholic sanctity". As he himself was at the time just on the point of becoming a Catholic this was singularly appropriate. She appeared, indeed, to be well fitted for the vacant angelic post. She was well educated, handsome, rich, a devoted follower of Cardinal Manning, who married them. Incidentally Patmore was not the sort of man to brook much influence from anyone over his wife, nor were the characters of the two men compatible and Manning, in spite of or perhaps because of Marianne's friendship with him, became "Poor Cardinal! It is wonderful how he imposed on mankind by the third century look of him and the infinite muddleheadedness which passed for mysticism."

The marriage was happy enough at first. The days of penury were over and Patmore settled down with zest to enjoy Marianne's riches. She was a good stepmother though she was never accepted by the two elder boys. But she was quiet and shy and had, before her marriage, contemplated becoming a nun, and such a character was only fitted to satisfy one side of Patmore's demands on a wife. Although he was fond of her there was never any question of her equalling the first "angel". As he put it with some crudity (alluding with a pun to Emily's fictitious name of Honor in the poem):

> I could not love thee, dear, so much
> Loved I not "Honor" more.

Gradually Marianne retired more and more into the background and Patmore's daughter, Emily Honoria, took her place. Emily the first had been a puritan who adored her husband too much to refuse him any gratification, though the "pale gold ground behind the little head" remained inviolate. This was the ideal Victorian "angel". It is ironic that her daughter, inheriting both her mother's puritanism and her father's mysticism to a heightened degree, should find her vocation in following a way of life which her mother would have regarded with horror. Emily Honoria became a nun and took her vows with enormous joy. Even more ironic is the fact that her father, who had drawn an analogy between earthly marriage and the union of the soul with God in that poem which had made him famous, was now forced to assent to his daughter becoming a veritable Bride of Christ. He fought against it. He took her to London for a season, he showered her with gifts among which was a diamond ring. But she dreamed away the days in reverie: listening to Madame Patti only made her wonder "that if a human voice can be so thrilling what must the voices of Angels be", and the ring she regarded as "a betrothal ring to our Lord". At last he gave in and even in time became reconciled and proud of her sanctity. He saw her frequently after she had taken her vows and she continued to be the companion of his heart until her early death. She read and discussed his poetry—and her reaction was not always that of unqualified admiration. She writes about *The Unknown Eros*, his second great work: "There are two lines in one ode that I could wish were not there. If I have said anything presumptuous, please forgive it."

If Emily Honoria's mother had reminded Browning of an early Italian madonna, possibly a Fra Angelico, she herself resembled a Leonardo da Vinci, intense, intellectual and flame-like. She was impatient for Heaven and burnt herself out after only a few years of convent life. She too fell a victim to consumption —though victim is hardly the word. When she was assured of a possible recovery she said quietly: "No, no! I am going to die." The joy she felt at the thought of death was ecstatic. What a contrast to the anxious regrets and careful planning of her mother. But she had neither children nor husband to provide for and even her regrets at leaving her father (for his sake not for hers) were lightened at the close.

During the last two years of Emily Honoria's life the second gentle devout Mrs Patmore had faded quietly away. Patmore built a church to her memory but he did not write any poems about her death; for some while before it had been fairly obvious that Harriet Robson, his younger daughter's governess, was to succeed as the third "angel". Emily wrote to her:

"Papa came the other day to tell me what I knew long ago . . . I am very glad . . . I have been praying long on the subject and I hope it is God's own arrangement for you and them all . . . I will pray hard these few days, and invoke for you such saints as the dear St Elizabeth and St Louis of France, who were so perfect in matrimony."

Harriet was young, energetic and lively. There are signs that she was satisfactory in just those ways in which poor Marianne had failed. She also gave him a son whom he loved far more than any of his other children except Emily. But there is no doubt that she was less angelic than her predecessors. She was no less adoring but she was very human. She suffered from jealousy and she was not one to keep her suspicions and grievances to herself. The letters between them show not only his physical dependence on her but her possessiveness.

> "My dear", he wrote, "yours would be a very wicked little letter if you really meant it, but I know you don't. I shall kiss all such perverse feelings out of you when I come back",

and again :

> "Don't be naughty, come on Monday by the early train. You are under obedience you know. Do not rebel."

The very idea of rebellion could not be taken seriously by the poet who wrote of the ideal wife :

> Her will's indomitably bent
> On mere submissiveness to him.

It is significant how often too the word "little" occurs in these letters to Harriet. Was it to conjure up "the baby smile"? In fact "little" was a favourite term of endearment with many a Victorian husband. Can one imagine Rosalind being addressed thus, or Imogen or Cordelia or Millamant ?

> "You have been for twelve years", another letter runs, "a thoroughly good and sweet little wife, and your trouble during the past few months, although it has greatly troubled me—makes me love you the more since it shows how much you love me."

Unfortunately this trouble was not without foundations for yet another and even more telling stroke of irony had befallen Patmore. This poet of the sanctity of marriage had, at the age of seventy-one, fallen desperately in love with the poetess Alice Meynell. Mrs Meynell, however, was not of the tribe of "angels in the house". She was an individual in her own right. Patmore himself realised that his former ideas would not fit this particular woman though he safeguarded himself and men in general by emphasising the rarity of such a being:

> "At long intervals the world is startled by the pheno-menon of a woman whose qualities of mind and heart seem to demand a revision of its conception of woman-hood and an enlargement of those limitations which it delights in regarding as essentials of her very nature and as necessary to her beauty and attractiveness as a woman."

It was most disturbing.

For four years the relation between the two poets grew in intensity, and on Patmore's side at least far beyond the bounds of friendship. Then Alice Meynell had had enough. This, for Patmore, was a totally new experience and a very bitter one, from which he never really recovered. He wrote to Francis Thompson, who was also emotionally involved with Mrs Mey-nell:

> "Dieu et ma Dame is the legend of both of us. But at present ma Dame is too much for the balance, peace and purity of my religion."

His last published writing was a review of her work and one of his very last letters, and a most characteristic one, was addressed to her:

> "My dear Lady,
>   I am dying . . . our meeting again in Heaven depends on your fidelity to the highest things you have known."

The story of Coventry Patmore and his three wives is an idyll of Victorian marriage. He is the poet who in *The Angel in the House* glorifies the love between husband and wife and, in the later odes which make up *The Unknown Eros*, he carries this glorification further—to a point even which was considered unpleasant. For the mystical eroticism of these odes was too naked and unashamed for Victorian taste, and they were as unpopular as his earlier work had been praised. Yet he had only one theme throughout—an analogy between the love of a husband and wife with that between God and the soul. In such an analogy the wife symbolises the soul and the husband God, and the significance of this symbolism is basic to Patmore's whole conception of the relation between the sexes.

2
Married to a Genius

Jane Carlyle
1801-1866

Much has been written about that uncomfortable couple, Thomas and Jane Carlyle. Their powerful, arrogant, grumbling, intolerant personalities still haunt the old house in Cheyne Road, Chelsea. Infuriating, yet fascinating, they invade most of the memoirs and correspondence of their times and their own copious letters bear witness for and against them:

"My heart has been steeped in solitary bitterness till the life of it is gone . . . Think of it, Jane! I can never make you happy."

"It is difficult for a young person of my attraction to lead the life of a recluse."

"Think not hardly of me, dear Jeannie. In the mutual misery we are often in, we do not know how dear we are to one another."

"You think, infatuated man that you are, that it is the greatest of hardships to have a home and a wife tied about your neck . . . but I consider it to have been a real blessing to you that you have been hindered in this way from bolting out into infinite space . . ."

—and so on and so on for forty-five troubled years. It is, then, impossible to write of marriage in the Victorian age and to escape them, and perhaps it may be of interest to examine their uneasy partnership in relation to the age and to consider how a different social pattern might have affected it.

Little, I imagine, would have changed Thomas. His health might have improved. He most likely suffered from gastric ulcers, yet, as it was, he lived to be eighty-six and was capable all his life of great exertion, so his constant indigestion and insomnia were probably mainly temperamental in origin and his temperament would have remained that of a highly neurotic genius, though the present century might have modified his attitude to women in general and to his wife in particular. But all women are more liable to be the victims of circumstances than men and with Jane Welsh Carlyle things might have been very different.

She was the only child of adoring parents. Her father especially found this sprite of a daughter, with her daring spirit and quick wits, irresistible. She should, he decided, be both son and daughter to him, should charm by her beauty but also should satisfy his need for intellectual companionship—for like many a clever man he had married a pretty but comparatively silly wife. But could a girl be safely educated up to this standard in those days? There were no precedents or traditions to help and Dr Welsh was guided only by ambition and possessive vanity.

The child, anxious to excel and above all to please her father, overworked outrageously. At ten years old Jane was often at school long before opening time when she was allowed to put in extra study. Not satisfied with this her father, although a doctor, actually engaged a tutor, Edward Irving (later to become a famous preacher), to coach her at home from six to eight every morning and again after school till bedtime. Irving was a brilliant young man and Jane was still further stimulated by him. He had to supply her father with a daily report and if this did not satisfy him she was reluctantly punished. The result of this early forcing was felt all her life, both physically in the form of frequent bad headaches and mentally because she involuntarily associated learning with anxiety to please and to be first. When it was feared that she would lack the accomplishments of a young lady she was consigned to the ordinary inefficient governess and finally to a finishing school. Her education and upbringing then was a muddle of different aims and experiments and, while feeding her vanity, failed to provide her with objective independent interests.

When Jane was nineteen her father died. She was overwhelmed by grief, and from that time on was in search of a substitute so that none of the young men who fell victim to her charm—for she was both fascinating and a flirt— managed to satisfy her.

It was not until she met Thomas Carlyle that she felt strongly attracted. But Carlyle, uncouth and of low birth, was on the surface so very unlike her handsome, gay, worldly-wise father, was so poor besides and so distasteful to her mother, that it took over five years from the time they first met to overcome all the obstacles to their marriage. These obstacles, too, were not on one side alone. Carlyle was deeply distrustful of himself and very shortly before the marriage was sending poor Jane the following encouraging love-letters:

"What is my love of you or of anyone? A wild peal through the desolate chambers of my soul . . . giving place to silence and death . . . I can never make you happy,"

and:

"I have been a very wicked man of late weeks . . . so splenatic, so sick, so sleepless, so void of hope, faith and charity; in short so altogether bad and worthless. I trust in Heaven I shall be better soon; a certain incident otherwise will wear quite an original aspect."

But Jane was accustomed to getting what she wanted and by this time she was certain she wanted Carlyle, so she replied: "For heaven's sake, get into a more benignant humour." It is to her credit that she could also write to a relative at the same time:

> "They would tell you, I should suppose, first and foremost, that my intended is poor . . . and in the next place most likely indulge in some criticisms scarce flattering as to his birth . . . and would to a certainty set him down as unpolished and ill-looking. But a hundred chances to one, they would not tell you he is among the cleverest men of his day, that he possesses all the qualities I deem essential in *my* Husband—a warm and true heart to love me, a towering intellect to command me and a spirit of fire to be the quickening starlight of my life . . . will you like him? no matter whether you do or not—since I like him in the deepest part of my soul."

Brave words, certainly true when they were written—true also to some extent throughout her life, but we are very mixed creatures and Jane and Thomas as mixed as any. They married in 1826.

In the first place Jane believed that it would be enough for her to fulfil herself through her husband and, as long as she could feel he really was dependent on her and achieving fame and recognition through her efforts, all was well, though it was uphill work subduing herself to the continual wear and tear of his despair, restlessness and self-pity. But in the first years of marriage she managed to be, on the whole, the meek and dutiful wife. They went to live on her ancestral farm at Craigen-puttock because he wished it, and they left it because he, after investing it with all sorts of romantic charms, found the reality harsh and isolating. She endured much but she never lost faith in his genius; indeed, having staked her whole life on it she dared not do so and it was certainly due to her clear sight and persistence that others too began to recognise it. It was she who realised that Carlyle must ultimately be based not in Scotland but London; it was she who insisted after the disastrous burning of the only copy of the first great volume of *The French Revolution* that it should at once be rewritten and it was this book that established his reputation. But she had, like many a hopeful bride before and after her, misjudged her influence in other ways. She was powerless before his moods and miseries, nor could the spoilt child and the gay Belle of Haddington remain for ever in abeyance.

Carlyle did not meet her half way. He seldom praised her or made much of her and he held "as an eternal axiom, the law of Nature that Man should bear rule in the home and not the Woman. It is the nature of man that if he be controlled by anything but his own reason, he feels himself degraded . . . It is the nature of a woman again (for she is essentially passive, not active) to cling to the man for support and direction, to comply with his humours and feel pleasure in doing so simply because they are his."

Yet, when it was necessary to cope with builders and decorators, with burglars, with noisy neighbours, even with income tax and tax commissioners, Jane's essential passiveness is apparently to be overcome for she had to do it all. To be sure, she, in common with nearly all her contemporaries, would have agreed with this analysis of the role of woman and for Jane Carlyle it held good; but for Jane *Welsh* Carlyle as she always insisted on being called, it was far from satisfactory. She was a very able woman, vain too and dependent for happiness on homage; she could not be content all her life with reflected glory. Carlyle was a natural solitary, he seldom demanded anything from her but to protect him from nuisance, to provide him with those meals which his incessant smoking and worrying made it impossible for him to digest, to listen to his grumbling and to amuse him, when he was in the mood, by her biting witticisms.

As his fame and prosperity increased she could no longer

feel that she had a part in it and she was by nature a sad misfit in the role of "angel in the house". She had to invent for herself some other satisfaction and sought it in the re-creation of an admiring circle such as she had been wont to reign over as a girl. Once they settled in London, this did not prove difficult. There is no doubt that Jane Welsh Carlyle possessed charm as well as wit. The latter is easy to recapture in her lively letters but charm is more fleeting and elusive than cleverness, beauty or goodness, and we catch ourselves wondering what it was in this self-centred and often waspish woman—"her tongue would take the skin off at a touch"—that subjugated so many men and women. There was integrity, there was sporadic but much real kindness, there was courage in a crisis, there was a glittering gaiety (but also moods of great gloom and self-pity) but there must have been besides some incommunicable delightful quality, such as called forth Leigh Hunt's pretty verse:

> Jenny kissed me when we met,
> Jumping from the chair she sat in;
> Time, you thief, who love to get
> Sweets into your list, put that in;
> Say I'm weary, say I'm sad,
> Say that health and wealth have missed me,
> Say I'm growing old, but add
> Jenny kissed me.

Some of her specially valued admirers were political exiles to whom she gave herself generously and whose obvious need of her was consoling. Of these Mazzini was the closest and dearest, but she treated him as her property and because she feared and resented any thing or person that distracted others from herself, she was never at rest, never satisfied. Indeed it must have been difficult to be at rest when married to a man who was given over to the determined pursuit of misery. "My life is black and hateful to me", seems to have been a frequent cry and when an inoffensive friend of Mazzini dared to speak of "the happiness of the people", "Happiness! Happiness!" stormed Carlyle, "The fools ought to be chained up."

Jane began to complain of him to her friends and she had another refuge—her ill-health. With increased fame and income came more headaches, more colds and influenza. "Jane Carlyle has eight influenzas annually," said Harriet Martineau. Yet when ill, a party was always able to revive her for the time being: "Last week I was all for dying . . . this week, all for Ball dresses." However ailing she became, she could not hope to outdo Carlyle in self-pity: "He has long since appropriated the chief right to raise an outcry . . . we are a grim pair living in an atmosphere far too sulphury and brimstonish." When not submerged in his writing Carlyle was unhappy, yet the writing itself was often an agony to him: "He is head over ears in Cromwell—is lost to humanity for the time being, fidgeting and flurrying about all the while . . . and writing every word with his heart's blood." She could not distract him or lighten the burden but after nearly twenty years of marriage she had to face the bitter fact that Lady Harriet Baring was able to give him all the distraction he needed.

Carlyle was an arch romantic. He was apt to see visions and dream dreams and it was no accident that he wrote in praise of hero-worship. Jane attracted him first as a bright being in another world from his own. But he never quite accepted her as she was. "O my darling," he exclaimed when he was getting to know her better, "were you but the being which your endowments indicate, with what entireness could I give up my whole soul to you. It is the earnest, affectionate, warm-hearted enthusiastic Jane that I *love*, the acute sarcastic, clear-sighted, derisive Jane I can at best admire. Is it not a pity you had such a turn that way." He wished her, in fact, to be other than she was.

Marriage, with its close day-to-day intimacy, is hard on the romantic to whom distance lends enchantment. "I understand," wrote Carlyle to a young friend, "what wonderful felicities young men like you expect from marriage, I know too that such expectations hold out but for a little while. I shall rejoice much if in your new situation you feel as happy as in the old, say nothing of happier." He found it easier with Jane to express affection and hope for the future when away from her.

As with wives, so with friends. Each new friend was marvellous, but the inevitable discovery of some defect too often was allowed to blot out all their good points.

Yet his nature craved for divinity, and in Harriet Baring, Lady Ashburton, he at last found someone he could worship, a strong personality with great natural gifts, glittering in an aristocratic sphere of her own, which allured him by its traditions, ease and nobility, into which he could enter but never dwell. It was the ideal situation. He adored her, addressing her as: "My Queen, my lamp in darkness"; "God bless you ever more, my Beautiful Lady"; "I have seen one royal woman in my life", etc., etc.

This was the most unhappy period in Jane's marriage. All day Carlyle would shut himself up with his writing and every evening he would rush off to Lady Ashburton. Now Jane was indeed thrown back upon her own resources and found them quite inadequate. She had never cared for knowledge for its own sake; the arts, except for a little popular music, meant nothing to either of the Carlyles. She had tried novel writing, about the only profession open to gentlewomen, but had had the sense to see that her gifts were not in that line.

To do him justice, Carlyle was sometimes aware that his wife had not enough to occupy her mind. When she was unusually depressed after her mother's death he had written:

> "My prayer is and always has been, that you would rouse up the fine faculties that are yours into some course of real work which you felt worthy of them and you. Your life would not then be happy, but it would cease to be miserable. It would become noble and clear with a kind of sacredness shining through it!"

That was all very well but far too vague to be of any use.

What could she do? Household management occupied her to a certain extent and the upheaval of replacing the fine Queen Anne panelling by painting and graining and putting in new windows, "the lower parts glazed with ground glass", and tearing out the old eighteenth-century fire-places for Victorian grates and constructing a sound-proof room for Carlyle, which proved not to be sound-proof at all—all this, in spite of ceaseless complaints of workmen and inconvenience, she obviously quite enjoyed. Servants were a continual obsession; she had thirty-four changes in thirty-two years. Friends were indispensable but they had to be devoted. Mazzini had defected, "having got up to the ears in a good twadley family of the name of Ashurst—who have plenty of money—and help 'his things' and toady him till I think it has gone to his head". But Geraldine Jewsbury, though often snubbed and slighted, was always to be relied upon and was the recipient of much bitter grumbling. Loneliness, jealousy and the desolate sense of failure resulted in more and more ill-health :

> "I struggle to keep my heart from throbbing up into my head and maddening it."

> "Alone this evening, Lady A. in town again and Mr C. of course at Bath House.

>> When I think of what I is
>> And what I used to was
>> I gin to think I've sold myself
>> For very little cas."

She lost her old self-confidence and, because she herself admired Lady Ashburton, she could not deride Carlyle's infatuation. She was always treated with courtesy and kindness by the great lady but felt unhappy and out of her element on the few occasions upon which she was persuaded to accompany her husband on a visit.

This sad and solitary period only came to an end with Lady Ashburton's death in 1857, "a great and irreparable sorrow to me", wrote Carlyle. "I have lost such a friend as I never had, nor am again in the least likelihood to have, in this stranger world." Jane's comment was: "I was shocked and dispirited and feeling silence best." By a curious and ironic fate, Lord Ashburton's second wife quickly became Jane's greatest woman friend, to whom she was about as devotedly attached as Carlyle had been to her predecessor.

Carlyle's last great book *Frederick the Great*, and named by Jane "The Valley of the Shadow", drove them both nearly mad. There was constant tearing of hair and changing of plans. "Poor Mrs Carlyle," says Lady Stanley, "who was going to Scotland Tuesday, has heard from the Philosopher that he returns to Chelsea like a cannon ball and so she goes to meet him. She is very amusing and tells no end of stories." For though life was exasperating, it never again took on such a desolating aspect. There were, indeed, not many years of this difficult partnership to run. An accident to Jane resulted in a more serious bout of illness than she had ever before experienced. "Poor Mrs Carlyle is very ill and nobody knows what is the matter with her. The doctors declare it is all on the nerves. She suffers dreadfully and her restlessness is worse than the pain", wrote Geraldine Jewsbury. This illness brought husband and wife closer. There was no attempt of course on either side at suppressing their dual misery:

> "Oh, my darling, ever since the day after you left, whatever flattering accounts may have been sent you—the truth is I have been perfectly wretched day and night with that horrible malady . . ."

> "Oh, my Husband! I am suffering torments, each day I suffer more horribly. Oh, I would like you beside me."

This was written from St Leonards where she had gone to

convalesce. From there, in spite of declaring that she had not slept at all for twelve nights, she travelled back to London and the next day took train to Scotland and slept well on arrival!

After six weeks she came back much better. The homecoming was savoured to the full. These incredible Victorians knew how to make the most out of their emotions. Carlyle rushes out in his dressing-gown to kiss and weep over her as she gets out of the cab, the maids (one of whom was given notice shortly after) greet her with tears and embraces, George Cook takes her in his arms and then sinks into a chair, Monkton Milnes likewise drops into a chair and bursts into tears "quite pale and gasping". Forster gives her great smacking kisses of joy and Woolmer "dropt on his knees beside my sofa and kissed me over and over with a most stupendous beard and a face wet with tears." Such a damp and rapturous reception did more for Jane than any medicine, and she was soon visiting her dressmakers, driving in her new brougham and writing to *her* Lady Ashburton—"O dearest of created ladies past and present and to come."

It is pleasant to dwell on these last two more peaceful years for Jane. Her friends seemed always at hand—Ruskin, the Frondes, Mrs Oliphant, Forster, the Stanleys, the faithful Geraldine—and she queened it among them as of old. Carlyle had at last done with Frederick and both he and she were much gratified when he was elected Rector of Edinburgh University. She did not go with him to the ceremony, giving as her reason: "If anything should happen to you, I find on any sudden alarm there is a sharp twinge comes into my back which is like to cut my breath and seems to stop the heart almost." Carlyle was too agitated and fussed at the thought of his speech to pay much attention. But he had a great triumph and she felt very proud of him: "I haven't been so fond of everybody and so pleased with the world since I was a girl."

Carlyle was away three weeks and Jane died of heart failure two days before his return. It was a good time to go. She had entirely recovered from the estrangement. She felt herself still loved by her crabbed old divinity and more than justified in her opinion of his genius.

Yet it is impossible in thinking of her life to avoid a sense of waste. She had intelligence and practical capability and spirit enough and to spare and she was aware of frustration. Her continual bad health was not only a legacy of early strain, it was a symptom which always lessened when she had occupation. She was angry with her brother-in-law who told her when she was ill that "if I had ever *done* anything in my life this would not have been", but her anger was reinforced by an inner suspicion that he may have been right. She had no children and there is good evidence that Carlyle was impotent. She herself appears to have been frigid. She was not a maternal woman; babies made no appeal to her with the one exception of the adored Lady Ashburton's little daughter. But none the less she may have felt this deprivation; the affection she poured over her dog Nero was significant. Yet the very thought of a child at Cheyne Row, and a child of two such parents, is staggering. Nero was a safe substitute for he made few demands and adored them both. In spite of Nero, however, there was a void in Jane's days and there was so little to show for them. She felt her life of dependence and vicarious satisfaction was all wrong: "If I have to lead another life in any of the planets I shall take precious good care not to hang myself round any man's neck either as a locket or a millstone!"

Geraldine Jewsbury and she used to discuss the problem, though Geraldine was more advanced in her ideas:

"I do not think that either you or I are to be called failures. We are indications of a development of womanhood which as yet is not recognised. It has, so far, no ready-made channels to run in, but still we have looked and tried, and found that the present rules for women will not hold us—that something better and stronger is needed . . . I regard myself as a mere faint indication, a rudiment of the idea, of certain higher qualities and possibilities that lie in women."

Jane today could have used her clear mind and clever fingers to good purpose in many different ways. She might have been an economist, or an outstanding journalist for, though she was unable to sustain a long narrative, her letters are full of witty and vivid descriptions. She could have returned to Carlyle fresh from her own particular world with mind and nerves far more able to cope with his, and he might have grown less self-absorbed, have managed even to invest her with some of that cloudy nobility his soul yearned for instead of terming her his "poor goody", his "necessary evil".

When they were at last engaged after five years of hesitation, Carlyle wrote: "Assuredly we cannot fail to be miserable and if we *must* suffer it is better surely that we should do so together than alone." It is an open question whether or no he was right. In many ways their mutual intolerance, hypochondria and moodiness seem to have been intensified by their partnership which probably might not have lasted long today. But certain it is that the Victorian ideas upon the whole duty of women were of no help at all to Jane Welsh Carlyle.

3
A Reluctant Rebel

Caroline Norton
1808-1877

Although her life spanned the greater part of Victoria's reign, the Honourable Caroline Norton, granddaughter of Richard Brinsley Sheridan, belonged by temperament and sympathies more to the flamboyant Regency period. Her family—Sheridans and Linleys, brilliant, gay, generous and improvident—had like leaping flames sprung into prominence, dazzling and warming all who came in contact with them, but faded all too soon. All the Linleys died young; so did Caroline's father, Tom Sheridan; so did her sons. Tom left, unprovided for, of course, three ravishing daughters of whom Caroline was the middle one famed at an early age for wit and determination. Her famous grandfather said of her that she was not a child he would care to meet in a dark wood.

The daughters' plain duty, in their penurious circumstances, was to marry as quickly and as well as possible. The eldest, Helen, obliged at the age of seventeen with Lord Dufferin's heir. Caroline, with her lovely Greek profile and enormous dark eyes, had already in her mid-teens caused some havoc among her male acquaintances. She was packed off to boarding-school where, through the introduction of a teacher related to Lord Grantley's agent, she met on an evil day at Wonersh Park this unpleasant peer's younger brother George, who fell immediately and violently in love with her. Caroline may have been flattered, she certainly was no more. Still, she was dowerless and in her second season at the age of nineteen she agreed to marry him. He was quite good-looking, of an ancient family, there was nothing against him as far as she knew, and her sister had told her that romantic feelings about one's husband before marriage were not necessary for happiness.

So this disastrous union took place. The two had nothing in common. George Norton was mean, avaricious, of a brooding, jealous temper, obstinate and slow. He was also very much in love. She was extravagant, romantic, quick-tempered, witty, generous and warm-hearted. Then there were their families, very much in the foreground, and equally diverse. The Nortons were cold, proud and quarrelsome, disliking each other only less than they disliked outsiders. They hated Caroline from the first and never forgave her her lack of dowry or the beauty with which she had subdued George. The Sheridans were devoted to one another and, finding that they had been misled by George as to his prospects, blamed themselves for letting Caroline marry such a disagreeable fellow.

Before we lose every shred of sympathy with Norton, as we soon must, let us see him for a moment as a lumbering dull creature bewildered and hurt by the brilliant wife whom he both adored and hated. For he had the wits to see very soon that she despised him and indeed her tongue did not spare him. She was never by nature a rebel. She required a husband whom she could revere and obey, for in this at least she was in tune with the age. She believed in the superiority of men but, alas, she found out soon after marriage that it was impossible for her to believe in the superiority of her particular man and there was no love on her side to soften the bitterness of the discovery. Nor could there even be affection between them where there was no sympathy or understanding. Exasperated by his inadequacy she indulged her wit at his expense and found that when angered he became violent. Probably for both there was a conscious or an unconscious wish for revenge, on his side for her disdain, on hers, for the physical outrage she must have suffered in a union with such a man. In her largely autobiographical novel, *Stuart of Dunleath*, the sensuality of the husband is stressed:

> "Of course he would be glad to inspire her with affection if he could, but if not, still let her be his—his at all hazards. This passion for her was as a bird of prey—Hope, tenderness, courtship, delay, were as little present in his thoughts as in the hawk that sweeps its circle and drops through the air. There are women who think it sublime to be loved with this sort of passion. The sublime of sensuality! It can be effaced as easily as the figures on a child's slate."

The birth of their first child, however, drew Caroline and George Norton together for a while. She was passionately maternal and he, too, according to his lights, was fond of his children. Incidentally the whole cost of the confinement was paid for by her out of proceeds from her first book of poems. But the calm could not last. Political animosity between the families flared up over the Reform Bill which the Whig Sheridans all supported and the Tory Nortons loathed. George lost his seat in Parliament and Caroline taunted him with his thick-skinned conceit: "He talks as though all those who voted against him did it with tears!" In 1833 when the birth of her third child was imminent a quarrel arose, trivial in itself, but ending in the husband breaking up the drawing-room furniture, forcing his wife downstairs and terrifying her utterly. But she was always quick to forgive and affairs were patched up.

About this time Caroline started a close friendship with Lord Melbourne, the Prime Minister. There is no doubt that this friendship was perfectly innocent on both sides. Melbourne never loved anyone but his wife, poor Caro Lamb, but he found the young, lovely and intelligent Mrs Norton stimulating company and she, who had always possessed political interests, rejoiced in his congenial companionship. Norton had no objection and accepted the office of a police magistracy which Melbourne procured for him. It is possible that, had it not been for the interference of Norton's sister and her friend—a Miss Vaughan, who appears subsequently to have been his mistress—the marriage might have settled down into an uneasy but respectable compromise. But the Sheridans and Nortons were like fire and water : they could not mix.

George's relations had never forgiven Caroline for her dowerless state and dismissed her beloved brothers and sisters as wild and improvident Whigs. The Sheridans, on their side, grew to dislike George Norton more and more for his behaviour to Caroline, and for his lack of any distinction or grace. They did not include him in an invitation to their sister and her children to share a holiday with them and at first he agreed that Caroline should go. But, at the last moment, his two evil attendant spirits so worked upon his jealousy that he withdrew his permission. Caroline, much distressed, left the house to discuss the matter with her relatives. On her return she found the children and their nurse locked away from her. There was a bitter scene and George's next move was to send away the children to the Nortons' home in Scotland. Neither passion nor pleading on the mother's part were of any use. Paternal rights were all-powerful and Caroline was not to see her little boys again for six months and then only for half an hour. It was six *years* before they were allowed to sleep once more under her roof.

When Meredith drew on Mrs Norton's story for his *Diana of the Crossways* he gave her no children, wishing, perhaps, to avoid the easy and obvious way of obtaining sympathy for his heroine. He wanted to draw attention to other wrongs and disabilities. Also by then, the worst injustices as to the custody of young children had been done away with owing in no small part to the exertions of Caroline Norton herself. But when George Norton, for no reason but that of personal spite, was able to inflict such misery on a devoted mother, she had no legal redress whatever. A married woman did not then exist at

42

all in the eyes of the law. She belonged to the category classed as "criminals, idiots, women and minors".

After the kidnapping of her children Caroline, not un-naturally, left her husband's house and sought refuge with her own family. In those days any wife who left her home, for whatever reason, was outlawed by society. Norton continued to live in the house which had been paid for by his wife's earn-ings and impounded all her jewels, books and clothes which he later tried to get her to buy back from him. Instigated by his family he then looked round for grounds for divorce. This was difficult, for though Caroline had had many and famous admir-ers, none was found to serve his purpose. At last Lord Melbourne was picked upon, chiefly because his political opponents thought there might be a chance of discrediting him and lent their support to Norton (who, by the way, continued to hold the post Melbourne had found for him, and later on tried to borrow money from him). However, the only two witnesses found for Norton were servants, formerly dismissed by Caroline for drunken unreliability and since maintained by the Nortons, and the case was concluded by a triumphant acquittal. Norton admitted that he had never believed in it, but he had not hesitated to defame his wife's name for, although Mel-bourne's reputation was entirely undamaged, a woman, who was by her sex disqualified from employing counsel to defend her, was bound to suffer from such an accusation however un-founded.

It was 1837—the reaction against the preceding age was in full swing. The sanctity of the family and above all of its male head was what mattered above everything and the highest possible standard of purity in women was exacted. Actual in-nocence was not enough; there must be avoidance of all contact whatever with any occasion for slander. As for "the branding iron of divorce", as a popular novelist* termed it, if there should be any implication of this a woman had only herself to thank: "She is a victim only to her own weakness or her own wicked-

* Mrs Jose.

43

ness." Even by breaking off an engagement a woman, according to Trollope, "has thrown off that wondrous aroma of precious delicacy which is the greatest treasure of womanhood*", and so late as Meredith's novels it is obvious that Clara Middleton feels that to take such a step would be disastrous. If a broken engagement could be viewed thus, how much more any connection whatever with a divorce trial.

Thus Caroline knew that, in spite of the acquittal, she could expect little sympathy from the public. She took refuge with a bachelor uncle, Charles Sheridan, whose friendship and whose home was unreservedly at her disposal until his death ten years later. But she was not one to retire into oblivion and all her energies were now directed towards obtaining access to her children and this depended entirely on her husband's consent, for though mothers were allowed custody of illegitimate children and also to retain their own property and earnings, all this was denied to the lawful wife. She cared nothing for Norton's stealing her purse or her good name :

> "If my children are kept from me, all else is trivial and indifferent . . . they may bereave me of my beloved boys (since the law allows it) they may drive me mad, or wear me into my grave by the slow torture of that greatest of sorrows; but while I have the control of my reason . . . I will sign nothing, do nothing, listen to nothing which has reference to any other subject—till it is decided what intercourse is to be allowed me with my children."

It added to her misery that they were under the care of someone who had always disliked her, who had accused her of mollycoddling them and whom she drew with a bitter pen in *Stuart of Dunleath* as "the mailed sister-in-law". She had, as transpired later, full justification for mistrusting the way the children were treated.

Fortunately for other wives and mothers she did not confine herself to private complaints and pleadings. She was determined

* 'Can you forgive her?'

not to remain passive under injustice and very soon after the trial she wrote a pamphlet challenging the law as it referred to the Custody of Infants. Serjeant Talfourd, roused by Caroline's case, brought in a bill to allow mothers, at the law's discretion, the charge of their children, if they should be under seven years old. This bill was passed in 1839 and, though it may seem a poor enough concession, it was a definite step forward and there is no doubt that Caroline's well-written pamphlet, privately printed and circulated to members of parliament, had much to do with its success. She produced this pamphlet without support. For, though it was not to bear her name, the Sheridans, for the first time, did not approve. Even they apparently were somewhat appalled at the challenge to the sacred prerogative of husbands and fathers. Nevertheless, she carried it through alone and what she did helped to change the law of England in women's favour.

In spite of the fact that after the trial Caroline was no longer received in many houses, such was the influence of the Sheridans and of her own charm that she was able to collect around her a small circle of staunch friends, for she loved society and this was one of the grievances between her and Norton. She was not immersed in her own trouble to the exclusion of others' needs. She had written and published at the height of these troubles the poem "A Voice from the Factories" in defence of the industrial child slave and she appears always ready to help her friends. Among these was Mary Shelley, the poet's widow, to whom she gave advice as to obtaining a pension for her unpleasant old father, the philosopher Godwin. She urged her to write with due humility to an influential personage : "As to not apologising for the intrusion," she says, "we ought always to kneel down and beg pardon for daring to remind people that we are not so well off as they are." Fanny Kemble, the actress, was one of Caroline's circle and declared of her : "She is a splendid creature, nobly endowed in every way." But she confessed anxiety "for a person so gifted, so tempted, in such a position as hers".

The children were still being kept in Scotland at the end of 1837 when George wrote a long letter to Caroline inviting her to come back to him. In this letter there is one casual allusion to the boys; all the rest is taken up with details of the wonderful bargains he has made in buying up articles of furniture which were for sale on the recent death of his mistress, Caroline's enemy. In her reply Caroline begs for news of her children. She does not refuse a reconciliation but makes it a condition that she should see the children at once. But it was spring again before at last they arrived after a year away. The baby, William, had been seriously ill but she had not been told and all three looked neglected and delicate. They were brought for short visits by their aunt. One day, Brinsley, the second boy, scarcely five years old, begged to stay the night with his mother. His aunt, inflamed by jealousy, threatened the child with punishment, upon which Caroline lost her temper with disastrous results. The children were not allowed to come again and when she rushed around to Norton's house she was refused entrance. They were removed to their uncle Lord Grantly's seat at Wonersh Park and having learnt that they were ill with measles, their mother followed them there and somehow managed to gain entrance to the nursery. While she was still with them Lord Grantly burst into the room, dragged the shrieking baby out of Caroline's arms and locked all the children away from her. Through shock and anxiety she became seriously ill but the Nortons ignored her doctor's plea that she should see or at least have news of her boys.

Now, however, public opinion began to veer round to her. She was even received by the young Queen. One point in Caroline's favour was that a Mr Bayley, Norton's former counsel at the trial, having been sent by him to treat with her, wrote: "Instead of finding her, as I thought but too likely, full of bitter animosity and revenge against you, I found her anxious to do everything . . . if it were only for the children's sake, to accede to your wishes in every respect. I found her extremely reasonable . . . and very forebearing. What I wish you to do now is to order your children to be brought up to London immediately . . . no *real* friend of yours would stand in the way." This last remark shows that Bayley was fully aware that it was Norton's family who were the fatal obstacle to any reconciliation. But his letter only resulted in a quarrel. Bayley became more and more favourable towards Caroline and even apologised to her for his part in the trial.

Meanwhile it was a grievous blow to discover that the children's living in Scotland put them outside the jurisdiction of the new Custody of Infants Act and that Norton could still refuse her access. She wrote pleading with him "for the sake of the days when the boys were a bond instead of a bitterness . . ." He put her off with continual promises which he failed to keep. Their rooms were made ready and fires were lit in them every day but still they never came.

> "You always speak as if the refusal of my boys was like a refusal of tickets for Almacks and that I was very rude and incourteous to take it so much to heart . . . *You* go about very carelessly and comfortably enjoying your usual occupations and doggedly settling in your own mind that, as the father of three fine boys, you have a legal right to torment their mother."

Next, the three children were sent to a particularly strict and rigid boarding-school in England. Caroline was refused the right to visit them there, but as a great concession they were allowed to spend part of the Christmas holidays with her. She took them on the last night to a play but because they had been seen with her in public, they were punished severely when they returned to the paternal roof. Then tragedy intervened. William, the youngest, now aged nine, died as the result of neglect after a fall from his pony. He asked for his mother twice but she was not told of his illness until it was too late. She arrived for the funeral and then, and then only, Norton agreed to let the remaining two boys live with her for six months in every year.

47

The reaction of the children to this reconciliation, as told in Caroline's letters, is moving. Our knowledge of psychology makes it the more poignant. Much in the social pattern of marriage has changed out of all recognition but for children the outrage of the broken home must remain unchanged.

> "Poor little Brinsley! he thinks having seen his father and me weeping together, all is once more peace and home. He made me write out a list of his relations of his Uncle Brinsley and George's children. He is full of eager anticipation to make friends of all that belong to me. He wrote to me 'I love you and my brother ten times more than I used to do. I love you, Papa and Spencer beyond anything I ever did before.' "

Of the elder boy, now aged thirteen, she says:

> "His whole care is to keep watch over his father's kindness that it may not flicker or go out. I think and hope that we shall now be very friendly together even if we continue apart . . . the children are so happy at being reknit to me that I can scarcely think of it without weeping."

It seems incredible that Caroline could forgive what had gone before, but hers was a temper that flared up, that lashed out, that spent itself and left her eager to forget and to be on good terms. Norton's was brooding and retentive and his love of money never let him rest where he thought an advantageous bargain could be made. The softer feelings which remorse had aroused in him were soon gone. He pretended to conclude a deed with her to pay her £500 in return for her signature to a Trust Fund for his family. She only discovered afterwards that this promise of his was invalid from the start as a wife could not legally contract with a husband. The case was taken to court and she was allowed to defend herself. "I do not ask for my rights", she pleaded, "I have no rights; I have only wrongs."

48

The court burst into cheers at her defence, but Norton won on some legal technicality. He continued to pay her no money for her keep, or the expenses she incurred for the children, nor was he bound to do so by law as long as she did not "come on the Parish". When the eldest son was seriously ill at Lisbon in 1848 and his mother went out to nurse him, she was left to pay everything and her husband also claimed all the income she made by writing. Melbourne on his death left her a small legacy and her mother soon after left her £480. Norton immediately attempted to appropriate these bequests.

In 1845, at the repeal of the Corn Laws, Caroline was again thrust into unwelcome prominence. She had become very friendly with young Sidney Herbert and a slanderous story was circulated that they had sold a premature announcement of the repeal to *The Times*. This was immediately and althoritatively denied by the editor. Sidney Herbert, like Melbourne, escaped scot-free from this calumny. On his side the friendship had not gone deep; indeed, he married soon afterwards. Men were allowed such distractions but once again the woman suffered from busy tongues. Caroline's own comment was only too true: "When a woman steps out of her domestic tangle to assert, because it *is* a tangle, her rights to partial independence, men sight her for their prey." Meredith seized on the story of Caroline and Herbert for the plot of his *Diana of the Crossways*, but in the novel she and she alone is portrayed as culpable. He wished to arouse sympathy for her as a guilty, not as an innocent victim, and apparently did not think of Caroline's good name. It is no wonder that her grandchildren objected and he agreed to put a foreword disclaiming the connection with Mrs Norton: "A lady of high distinction for wit and beauty, the daughter of an illustrious Irish House, came under the shadow of a calumny. It has latterly been examined and exposed as baseless. The story of 'Diana of the Crossways' is to be read as fiction."

The feud with Norton continued and now Caroline wrote another pamphlet arraigning the law. This time, following a succession of injudicious letters to *The Times*, the production was far too long and emotional to have the desired effect. In 1854 a most inadequate bill to reform divorce was brought forward but, owing in part to the outbreak of the Crimean War, was laid aside, and in 1855 Caroline produced a third and much more influential tract entitled *A Letter to the Queen*. This restrained and powerful appeal was the only one of her three pamphlets to be produced under her own name and published openly. It was favourably acclaimed and Lord Broughton declared that "he believed it would result in a much amended law". This indeed proved to be the case.

The address first stresses the anomaly that a married woman reigns over a country whose laws ordain that married women shall be non-existent:

> "As her husband, he has a right to all that is hers: as his wife she has no right to anything that is his. As her husband he may divorce her (if truth or false swearing can do it): as his wife, the utmost divorce she could obtain is permission to reside alone—married to his name. The marriage ceremony is . . . an indissoluble sacrament for her; the rights of mutual property are made absolute for him and null for her . . . the religious vow taken by the man in marriage is merely to give him civil rights over the woman."

The *Letter* continues with a reference to a speech of Gladstone's when he declared that Christianity put woman on an equality with men but, said Mrs Norton, "a sneer is the only answer to Mr Gladstone's gospel doctrine and the only text on the subject acknowledged by Parliament is the Old Testament text 'and he shall rule over her'."

The Scottish law allowed women to divorce for adultery and in an amusingly ironic passage Caroline, quoting the House of Lords' decision that to permit women to have this privilege "would be productive of the grossest immorality", draws a picture of Scotland as "a hotbed of vice, dedicated to Cupid with statues of Venus set up in all the principal squares of Edinburgh", and says that: "whilst your Majesty is surrounded with faithful wives and discreet ladies in London, Windsor and Osborne, the less cautious portion of the realm in which Balmoral is situated is plunged in the grossest immorality."

This was actually taken seriously by the *Caledonian Mercury* who attacked Mrs Norton for libel. When their mistake had been pointed out, they apologised and she immediately and with characteristic generosity wrote: "I am quite sure I must have written the passage badly."

The pamphlet declares with truth that cheating at cards, or a debt of honour, would have put all England against Mr Norton at once but

"What is all this disturbance about? Women's rights and women's wrongs? pooh, pooh, nonsense; Bloomerism;* Americanism! We can't have that sort of thing in England. Women must submit, those who don't are bad women—depend upon it; all bad women."

Caroline makes it quite clear that she is not rebelling against what she believes is "of God's appointing" the natural inferiority of women:

"I never pretended to the wild and ridiculous doctrine of equality . . . Put me then (my ambition extends no further) in the same position as all Mr Norton's other inferiors—in that of his housekeeper whom he could not libel with impunity, of an apprentice whom he could not maltreat lawlessly, of a scullion whose wages he could not refuse, of a labourer with whom he would not argue that his signature to a contract is worthless."

* A term derived from the fashion of wearing a sort of trouser costume adopted by some advanced women in America and named after a Mrs Bloomer.

The *Letter* ends with a renewed plea for support to the Queen, as the "one woman in England who *cannot* suffer wrong", and with a vow

> "to abjure all other writing till I see these laws altered . . . I deny that this is my personal cause; it is the cause of all the women in England.
>
> "Meanwhile my husband has a legal lien on the copyright of my works. Let him claim the copyright of this and let the Lord Chancellor cancel in Mr Norton's favour my right to the labour of my own brain and pen; and docket it among forgotten Chancery Papers . . . 'Only a woman's pamphlet'."

This was *not* the fate of the *Letter to the Queen*. It aroused great interest and discussion and two years after its publication a much amended Divorce Bill became law. This provided a deserted wife protection from claims on her earnings—it ensured that a wife might inherit and bequeath property and it gave a separated wife power of contract and of sueing and being sued in any civil proceeding. The first steps towards giving women legal status had been taken.

The rest of Caroline Norton's life hardly concerns us. She made new friends: Motley, the American historian, who described her to his wife as having had "a most dangerous terrible beautiful face in her prime and is very handsome still"; Sir William Stirling, a kindly scholar whose two little boys she amused by making them model castles in cardboard and who called her Aunt Marmalade. Her eldest son died at the outset of a promising diplomatic career of the Sheridan family scourge, consumption; the second one married an Italian peasant girl in Capri and sent his two children home to the guardianship of the mother who for six years had been legally deprived of her own sons. Norton died and, as by then Sir William Stirling was a widower, she tasted of married happiness at last with this gentle humorous man. But it ended so swiftly: it was only a few months after their marriage in 1877 that Caroline died. She left a reputation that was full of light and shade. She was not a true feminist, she claimed protection from the law, not equality. For this reason she was never accepted or approved by the more objective and committed women of her time, such as Harriet Martineau. They saw that had she been less unfortunate, she would have remained silent. She sums up her own marriage with bitter truth: "By resisting him I made him a tyrant and he by insisting made me a rebel."

So she became a reformer in spite of herself. With any luck she might have been a successful and contented wife, instead she was blamed and shunned for her notoriety, for her wit and even for her proud beauty. But she was also loved and admired and pitied and she turned her sufferings to good account. She won the first battles for Victorian wives against outrageous and cruel laws.

4
Two Breadwinners

Frances Trollope
1780-1863

The lot of a Victorian wife was peculiarly hard when the ivy
had to prop up its tower while, for society's sake, still presenting
the appearance of the tender parasite plant. There is an irony
that this image of the "ivy and the tower" should have pro-
ceeded from the pen of Frances Trollope's son, whose family
had been supported by her efforts when the tower had crumbled
into a ruin. There is irony too in the letter of proposal which Mr
Trollope wrote her. It is very long. The Trollope family were
never sparing of words, and the greater part is taken up with a
detailed statement of his property and prospects. In its style
and approach it is an interesting period piece :

"My dear Madam.
   "In the course of last Spring, I was no little delighted
with the subject a certain debating society had chosen for
their weekly discussion, which, to the best of my recollection, was in the words, or to the effect following :
   " 'Is it most expedient for a man to make an avowal of
his attachment to a lady viva voce, anglice tête-à-tête, or by
epistolary correspondence?' What the determination was
that these learned orators came to upon a question that
must have been so interesting to all unmarried men, did not
reach me; neither is it of consequence to me upon the

present occasion. But my reason for adverting to this proposed debate, is because I well remember, and probably, my dear madam, you may also, that there was one, altho not of this honourable Society, who expressed a most decided opinion upon the subject; and to that opinion I now think myself bound to submit. To me, I must confess that the question appeared to be calculated to afford an ample field for declaration, and to be attended with considerable difficulty, but I believe that the only observation I made at the time was that which Sir R. de Coverley found so convenient and apposite upon almost all occasion : 'Much was to be said on both sides of the question.' And indeed, having discovered your sentiments, and having no occasion to waste any further thoughts upon the subject, my mind, I confess, continues much in the same state of dubriety.

"In submitting therefore to your opinion I am making no sacrifice of my own, altho had the sacrifice been necessary your ideas, as they ought, would have been the sole guide of my choice.

"I had little thought, my dear Madam, that this preface would have run to so considerable a length; since, however, it explains the motive of my now addressing you, it will save me the necessity of a more explicit avowal, and sufficiently declare to you that my future happiness on earth is at your disposal.

"It is impossible but that I must feel every anxiety till I am favoured with your reply to this note, yet I shall say nothing under the hopes of accelerating it. If, indeed as I trust is the case, you are not entirely unaware that my chief delight has long since had its source in your society and conversation; and if, permit my vanity to indulge the hope, there has been the slightest degree of mutuality in this delight, then perhaps—I confess I scarcely know what I was going to say, but perhaps you would not require *three weeks* for passing a sentence on

which I must so anxious depend. Many circumstances however, I know, must and indeed ought to be taken into
consideration before this serious, this final step can be
resolved upon. There is no one perhaps that has a greater
contempt for those who are induced to contract alliances
upon motives of a pecuniary nature than I have; but at the
same time I have had experience enough to teach me that
happiness is not to be expected where the parties are no
longer capable of enjoying those necessaries and comforts
of life to which they have been accustomed, and which
are commonly incident to the rank and situation they hold
in Society."

There then follows as much again setting out the details of
his income, expectations and incumbrances and the letter ends:

"I must now draw this long letter to a conclusion . . .
my sole object has been to make a declaration which I
could no longer conceal and at the same time to state those
circumstances, a knowledge of which, in case you think
the subject of my writing worthy your consideration,
would be necessary for that purpose. In doing this in the
most simple manner and in rejecting the flippant nonsense
which I believe to be commonly used on occasions of this
nature, I doubt not I have acted as well in conformity
with your sentiments as those of

My dear Madam—your sincere admirer
and most devoted servant,
THOMAS ANTHONY TROLLOPE"

Poor Mrs Trollope, there is evidence that she would have
enjoyed a little of that flippant nonsense which he so much
despised. In the early days of her marriage she confesses: "I
own my heart welcomes a look or a word of fondness from
those who are dear to me, as cordially as it does more unequivocal proof of attachment"—and at the end of the letter: "Adieu,

my very dear husband (I was going to write 'dearest' but recollected that your correctness would laugh at me)."

Trollope was an unattractive pedant, honest and industrious and a scholar but hopelessly impractical and difficult to get on with. It was unfortunate that his expectations of an independent fortune from an uncle were disappointed; but his failures as a barrister, a business man and a farmer were due to a lack in the man himself. He became soured by misfortune though he had never been of a cheery disposition and, probably from psychological causes, he grew to be a martyr to severe headaches. With that curious attraction of opposites sometimes operative between the sexes, he had chosen as his wife a woman of an extraordinarily buoyant and sanguine disposition. Neither of them however had any common sense.

The Trollopes' early married life was happy enough. They lived at Pinner where Frances had congenial friends. Children arrived (seven altogether of whom four died of consumption before they reached the age of twenty) and she was fond and proud of them, especially of the eldest, Tom. But her husband's own thwarted ambition was very soon to centre on these children and poison their happiness. He began to give Tom and Henry Latin lessons before breakfast, from the ages of five and four respectively, and Emily on her seventh birthday, by way of a treat, had been "taken through a very good sum in vulgar fractions". The two boys were sent to Winchester and their mother was forced to write: "Tell Henry no cake shall be sent until his father can have a better account of his industry. You, my dear Tom, must also partake in this loss, but I shall know how to make amends."

The partially disillusioned wife is beginning to centre her life round her eldest son: "When you are next at home I shall insist upon your going with me to the National Gallery. It begins to be worth seeing and I begin to be anxious to find out whether you are like to enjoy the pleasure which a good picture is capable of bestowing." She also looks forward to reading Italian with him.

Meanwhile Trollope's practice as a barrister was going from bad to worse and, knowing nothing about farming, he decided to take this up as an alternative career.

The Trollope children suffered greatly from their parents' lack of common sense. When Henry was just fifteen and still making little progress at Winchester, they took him away from school and left him to fend for himself in a Paris counting house. It was twelve years after Waterloo and he wrote: "When I am walking it is not uncommon to hear the boys holloa out 'Voici le petit goddam! Nous battons les Anglais avec des manches à balai'."

Henry, not unnaturally, continued to be an anxiety; and also, not unnaturally, the experiment in farming was failing and was succeeded by a still more impractical plan. Trollope invested what remained of his capital in building a shop or bazaar for fancy goods in Cincinnati. He had heard that English goods obtained cheaply in England would find an easy and productive market in the States and this shop, or some similar opening, would also provide employment for Henry. It was decided that Mrs Trollope with Henry and her two little girls should make the hazardous journey and get things going, to be joined later by Trollope and Tom. Eventually Henry was to be left in charge, and the rest of the family would return to England.

Another factor which influenced the Trollopes at this time was a meeting with an American lady, a Miss Wright. Miss Wright was an idealist possessed of ample means and gift of persuasion. She was a ward of General Lafayette, wore the newly invented "Bloomers" and had written a successful book about Athens. She was an enthusiastic advocate of race equality and had decided to devote her fortune to establishing a Utopian community in a forest settlement near Memphis, where Negro and white children were to be educated together. The name of Harmony was to be given to the settlement and Henry was to finish his education there as a sort of pupil teacher. A young Frenchman, M. Hervieu, was also enrolled by Miss Wright as an art teacher and full of excitement the whole party set off to sail from London in the autumn of 1827. They arrived after a voyage of nearly two months and made their way to Harmony. But, alas, one look at Miss Wright's Utopia was enough: "Desolation was the only feeling—the only word that presented itself, but it was not spoken. I think, however, that Miss Wright was aware of the painful impression the sight of her forest-home produced on me." The Trollopes spent only ten days at Harmony. Among other drawbacks the climate was unhealthy for white settlers and this factor eventually defeated even Miss Wright's enthusiasm.

After this unfortunate start the family made their way to Cincinnati and now indeed Mrs Trollope found that the delicate creeper could no longer rely on any sort of wall at all, let alone a strong one. No letters reached her for six months after leaving England and, worse still, no money.

"I cannot express to you the dreadful anxiety to which this silence gives birth", she wrote to Tom. "Is your father ill? Is he dead? Have his affairs fallen into such confusion that he has not been able to procure the money necessary to send us a remittance? Our situation here would be dreadful were it not for M. Hervieu's generous kindness. It is more than a month that we have not had a mouthful of food that he has not paid for. Dear Tom, dear Anthony, do not forget us! . . . You would hardly know Henry and me, we are both grown so thin."

Tom and Anthony were during this period both at Winchester together. Mrs Trollope was perhaps no more hopelessly wrong about her boys than many mothers. When Anthony first joined Tom at school she wrote: "How greatly comforted am I to know that Tony has a perfect brother. I well remember what I used to suffer at the idea of what my little Tom was enduring." But, according to Tony's own bitter memories in the autobiography, this perfect brother "was, of all my foes, the worst . . . As part of his daily exercise, he thrashed me with a big stick." It must be conceded, however, that such thrashings were apparently part of the accepted order of things. But worse was to follow for poor Tony, for Tom left and went with his father to Cincinnati and no one paid the school bills. Tony became a pariah and, "ill dressed, dirty" and cruelly treated by his schoolfellows, he even contemplated suicide.

Meanwhile Trollope's visit to Cincinnati only added to his dismal record. The bazaar, like his law practice and his farming, proved a complete failure. Not all the consignment of shoddy goods shipped from England could save it. Nor could the magnificent folly of the building, which a contemporary described as "a large Graeco-Moresco-Gothic-Chinese looking erection—an architectural compilation of prettiness of all sorts!" By the time he and Tom embarked for home after a five months' stay, it was obvious that the only course was to get rid of the affair as soon as possible. Mrs Trollope was left to cope with the situation as best she could. Tom went to college and Tony was taken from Winchester to live with his father in a tumble-down old farmhouse near Harrow School, where he was sent as a day-boarder. Dirty, uncared for, half-starved, despised and outlawed by his schoolfellows, with a mother who was far away and a father whose sole attention to him seems to have been to see that he sat with his school books in front of him for a certain period a day, he led a pitiable existence.

Trollope was not cruel, he simply did not believe that anything but Greek, Latin and mathematics was necessary for a growing boy. Even in this he went hopelessly astray. "No father was ever more anxious for the education of his children," wrote Anthony, "though I think none ever knew less how to go about the work." For some reason Tony was the child Mrs Trollope cared for least; he was certainly the only neglected one, yet he was the most like her in temperament and gifts. Had he possessed a less resilient spirit, he could never have developed into the cheerful, successful civil servant, and novelist after such a boyhood.

While Mr Trollope and his youngest son were dragging out a miserable existence at Harrow, Mrs Trollope was enduring penury and illness at Cincinnati. She turned more and more to

Tom: "Alas, since we last conversed together, my life has been almost one continual scene of suffering. Often have I rejoiced that you were where you could not see it. Yet often would I have given much to have your affection to support me." It was the only support she was likely to get. She and Henry both became ill, no money was forthcoming from home and again she wrote to Tom in desperation:

> "In one letter, in answer to one of mine in which I stated our situation, your father writes—'How is it possible that you are dependent on Hervieu for your living when I have sent out goods to the amount of £2,000?' Is it not strange, Tom, that he does not yet know that those goods never brought *one penny* into my hands? The proceeds of those we sold went to workmen and servants and the rest was seized . . . I would have you recall this to his memory. Poor Cecilia is literally without shoes and I mean to sell one or two small articles to-morrow to procure some for her and for Emily. . . . As to other articles of dress we should as soon think of buying diamonds. Your dear sisters have had a pretty sharp lesson in economy. They mend and mend and mend."

Yet it may be noted as a matter of interest that even in such straits the family was never without a servant. At first there were some regrettable instances but then—"notwithstanding I had the dread of cooking my own dinner, before I would take any more 'young ladies' into my family I resolved upon receiving some slight sketch of their former history. At length I met with a very worthy Frenchwoman, and soon after with a tidy English girl to assist her." These two she kept until she was ready to leave for England. Shoeless and in near rags the family might be, but to be servantless was unthinkable for a middle-class Victorian wife.

But after she recovered from her illness, with the full realisation of her husband's uselessness, Mrs Trollope's own resolution and resource came to her rescue. She determined to turn this unfortunate venture to good account after all. She would write a book about her experiences in America though she was over fifty and had never written before in her life. She set to immediately and, with a characteristic wry humour, declared that she was at least saving shoe leather for "I sit still and write, write, write, write." Neither then nor later did she receive the slightest encouragement from her husband, who was convinced from the first that the book would be a failure. Perhaps he had forgotten to think in any other terms, perhaps he subconsciously shrank from the reversal of the right and proper order of the universe that would follow should the parasite become the prop. His wife brought the finished book back with her when she returned to England in 1831 after having been away four years. It was published immediately and was an immense and lucrative success. From then onwards she and she alone supported the family.

The Domestic Manners of the Americans, besides being Frances Trollope's best book, is the only one that is remembered today. Its success owed much to the fact that, like Dickens's *American Essays* and *Martin Chuzzlewit*, it was highly controversial, arousing strong feelings on both sides of the Atlantic. But this was not the whole secret. Frances Trollope had no profundity of thought, her judgements were superficial, always prejudiced and sometimes silly, but she had a seeing eye and a lively pen. The glorious strange beauty of a virgin country with its alien vegetation and wild life appealed strongly to her, and she spent the last year of her time in the States travelling. Her descriptions are never boring; she makes us see the lonely clearings and farms, the huge silent rivers, Niagara, untamed and unvulgarised, the clear bright air, "the exquisitely lovely" approach to the New York of those days, with its spacious gardens and pretty houses. New York itself—"much less thickly peopled than Paris", well-planted with trees "and with buildings of a beautiful stone, called Jersey freestone of a warm rich brown."

Such descriptions have for us now a historical interest but then, any travel book was a novelty and especially one written by a woman. But although this alone would have probably ensured publication and a moderate success, the phenomenal sales of the book were undoubtedly due to the criticism of American outlook and customs. We should not expect to find a balanced unprejudiced view for a good many reasons. First, it was only fifteen years since England had been at war with the United States of America and the earlier and more important War of Independence was still fresh and bitter in memory. Secondly, Mrs Trollope was a staunch Tory, at heart conventional and fearful of change; the idea of democracy was abhorrent to her. Thirdly she was very unhappy while in America. It was here that the disillusionment with her marriage became fatally clear and was all the harder to accept because of her innate conformity.

It is interesting that American reviewers recognised that the book was "conceived in bitterness, evidently indicative of personal disappointment". They attack, with justice, generalisations drawn from an unfortunate experience and in one particular district—that of Cincinnati, "a region, half-civilised"—her knowledge of other districts being formed on a hasty visit only. "It is to be regretted that she holds up as the make and model of a great people the drunken boatman of a frontier river, or the ditcher of some interior canal," wrote one critic. Such generalisations as Frances Trollope's are a common fault of the traveller. The *American Quarterly Review* draws a clear distinction, which was evidently held at the time, between the "destitute myriads of foreigners" or "the squatter, the poor defeated adventurer from another state in these least cultivated and settled regions" and the true pioneers, "who have gone singing cheerily into the gloomy forests", and upbraids Mrs Trollope for not making the same clear distinctions. She has failed to appreciate what America "has done in the teeth of poverty, the oppression and privations of two protracted wars with a nation whose boon and birthgift was the stepdame's curse."

On the whole the *American Quarterly* enjoyed itself reviewing Mrs Trollope and it is certainly as fair a review as can be expected, even agreeing with her strictures on tobacco chewing and spitting and the separation of the sexes in society. The *North American Review* is concerned to show up the far worse domestic manners of the English in the slums of London and Manchester but the *New English Magazine* admits that there is generally some foundation even for caricature and that though Mrs Trollope describes individuals as a class and travelled to find fault, "if we will not look at the picture which enemies make of us, we may never be acquainted with our own peculiarities." But it was impossible that bitterness should not have been widely felt and indeed, when Tom Trollope was later contemplating a journey to the States, he was advised to travel under another name.

At home, the *Edinburgh Review* called the book "ill considered and mischief making" but the majority sided with the rival *Quarterly* who praised it highly. In an interview with Murray on the subject of the possible publication of one of his own erudite manuscripts, Mr Trollope was called back with a "By the bye, Trollope, who the devil *is* this Mrs Trollope? Her book is the cleverest thing I ever read, so spirited. It will sell like wildfire." It did, and on the proceeds the Trollopes were enabled to leave the tumble-down old house and move to a charming one which her son has immortalised as Orley Farm.

But the wage-earner had no intention or indeed any chance of resting on her laurels. She continued to write hard, carrying this on almost entirely before breakfast. For the rest of her time she led a lively social life and acted, as of old, as mediator between father and children. Trollope could never bear to allow his sons any money. Even when, as now, Tom was doing well with a small exhibition at Oxford, he was expected to live on £15 for the whole quarter and to save at least £4 to bring back with him. It might be supposed that she who paid the piper would call the tune. But this rarely followed in Victorian society between husband and wife, where anyway all the wife's earnings became legally and as a matter of course the property of the husband. Trollope, too, was obsessed with the idea that he might compensate for his financial failures by severe austerity imposed on himself and his family, so that unnecessary hardships were imposed on his family and himself to the detriment of health as well as happiness.

Thus, after an absence, Mrs Trollope returned to find "Tom lying in a comfortless garret without a pillow under his poor aching head. You know that not one of our five children has a pillow for their heads." The frequent rows between Henry and his father were so severe that they reduced the mother to extreme agitation so that she had to take laudanum. But relief came in the shape of "a full and compendious explanation of all ecclesiastical rites and ceremonies, a distinct and accurate account of all denominations of Christians from the earliest ages of Christianity to the present time, together with a definition of terms usually occurring in ecclesiastical writers". Just the ticket for Mr Trollope; it might also have attracted Mr Casaubon. "I cannot express my delight", wrote Mrs Trollope to Tom, "at his having found an occupation. He really seems quite another being and so am I, too, in consequence."

This kept the man of the family out of the way, though it did not cure his headaches, nor did it undo the mistakes of the past and, after the bright patch that succeeded the success of the American book, clouds began to gather. In spite of his wife's unremitting labour, debts piled up and blunders and omissions, extraordinary in a legal man, came to light. Mrs Trollope's marriage settlement had never been registered. Title-deeds of property lodged as securities were found not to have been acknowledged and so irreparable losses were incurred. Henry's health was giving great anxiety and then suddenly, Mr Trollope disappeared and the bailiffs descended upon the home. Mrs Trollope did not tell Tom of this latest blow until he had taken his finals—then she wrote: "Nothing surely of equal importance was ever left in such a manner (unless it was the bazaar at Cincinnati). I have done and will do all I can to set things in order. But I must see, and talk to you before you can have an idea of how everything has been left."

The family reassembled at Bruges and now followed the most heroic period of Mrs Trollope's married life. She had an exacting and extremely irritable patient in poor Henry, a husband whose health and spirits were quickly deteriorating, a hobble-de-hoy schoolboy son of whom little was expected, and two delicate daughters. The day was taken up with nursing and housekeeping and during the greater part of the night she kept herself awake with strong coffee, and wrote for all their livelihoods. Tom had found himself a teaching post in Birmingham and so was not with her to provide support. At last at the end of this fearful year Henry died. He was the third of the children to suffer from tuberculosis and she was to lose two more and two grandchildren from the same disease. Anthony then obtained a minor appointment at the Post Office through one of his mother's relatives, and a successful book on Paris was published which was attacked even more fiercely than *The Domestic Manners of the Americans* and sold equally well. It, too, was strongly anti-democratic.

In February 1835, the poor ruined tower finally fell. His son wrote of him: "We were all estranged from him, and yet I believe that he would have given his heart's blood for any of us. His life as I knew it was one long tragedy, the touch of his hand seemed to create failure.'

It was certainly true that after Trollope's death nothing was ever so difficult for his wife again but there was plenty of sadness still, for the younger daughter, Emily, was the next victim and after they returned to England the same heartbreaking period of hopeless nursing followed. There are some natures which are constitutionally unfit for tragedy. It is not that they are unfeeling but that they can shed sorrow like a shower of raindrops shaken from a flower that then turns towards the sun. Frances Trollope loved her children deeply, even more because her husband had failed her so hopelessly, yet her buoyant spirit, which lived very much in the present, overcame the triple bereavement of this fatal year and the next year we find her voyaging on the Danube from Ratisbon to Vienna "in a week of heavy rain", sleeping every night in miserable dirty quarters but ending up in full glory at the Austrian court—a glory which shed its beams as far as Mrs Browning's Wimpole Street couch where she lay writing to Miss Mitford: "Not Mrs Trollope on the right hand of Prince Metternich could rejoice more in la crème de la crème than does my Flushie." A book on Vienna inevitably followed and more and more novels, for a livelihood still had to be earned as, truth to tell, Mrs Trollope was inclined to be extravagant, and after the extreme austerities of her husband who shall blame her? There is little of lasting merit in these books. *The Vicar of Wrexhill* (1837), which had the honour of being quoted once by Sydney Smith, gives an unpleasant picture of an evangelical clergyman, a foreshadowing of Mr Slope in *Barchester Towers*. *Michael Armstrong, the Factory Boy*, published in serial form in 1839, was admired by Dickens and Lord Ashley and testifies to Mrs Trollope's warm heart. It contains one or two vivid passages on the horrors of child labour. *The Blue Belles of England*, a satire on the fashionable marriage market, was "very clever" in Mrs Browning's estimation, but the other hundred or so books churned out by her pen are totally forgotten.

In the latter part of her life she relied more and more on Tom, who came to live with her in Florence until he married. She appears to have led a happy social life though the Brownings, Baring Gould, the novelist, and Mrs Lynn Linton considered her a little vulgar. Possibly, the ivy, having trailed in the dust of a fierce economic struggle, had lost some of that delicacy so prized by the Victorians. And the struggle was not yet over. Cecilia, the married daughter, fell ill in her turn of the dread disease and her mother, now sixty-nine, went to London to nurse her. With sad familiarity we read a letter to her publisher: "What to do about my book I know not. The difficulty of finding a quiet half hour here to write is incredibly great. Sometimes I feel in absolute despair on the subject. At night, the only quiet time (though I am sorely tired), I *would* try had I but a fire to sit by."

She weathered this last blow and lived on another thirteen years. Her last words give the lie to any reproach of heartlessness. They were not of her two successful sons, nor of her books or fame, but of this daughter—"Poor Cecilia".

Anthony Trollope sums up his mother's character and achievements thus:

> "Her books saved the family from ruin. She was an unselfish, affectionate and most industrious woman, with great capacity for enjoyment. She was endowed with much creative power . . . But she was neither clear-sighted nor accurate and was unable to avoid the pitfalls of exaggeration."

These are just the defects which a sound education might have corrected but the Victorian wife had had no opportunity for a sound education.

Margaret Oliphant
1828-1897

Margaret Oliphant, like Mrs Trollope, was forced to fill a role which was the exact opposite of that which society considered natural and proper for a wife and mother. In her case she was the sole prop and support of no less than five parasite males who lived upon her unremitting labour and, moreover, this regular professional work was all carried out after her ordinary authorised womanly duties had been duly accomplished each day. "I don't think I have ever had two hours undisturbed for writing except when everyone else is in bed during my whole literary work", she wrote in old age. Henry James called her "a night-spinning spider of long, loose, vivid yarns". They might well have been less long and loose and more enduring had her circumstances been easier, for she had marked talent and unlike Frances Trollope was a born writer, beginning young, and for the joy of it.

By her early twenties she had published two tales and she had been introduced to the great Christopher North of *Blackwood's*. He had not taken her seriously, of course: "As long as she is young and happy work will do her no harm," he remarked benignly, unaware of the irony of his words, for this girl was more than any other to maintain the tradition of his beloved "Maga"* and to do so throughout a life of much toil and tragedy.

* The famous *Blackwood's Magazine* was known as "Maga" for many years.

Young though she was at the time, it is characteristic that in her second story she refused to succumb to the pressure of her august publishers to sentimentalise the portrait of Bonny Prince Charlie. She did not see him like that and would not alter anything. "It may be that I judge wrongly", she wrote to them, "still I *do* judge and as it is an honest opinion this must stand as it is."

The cheque which she earned for her first story had been spent in travelling to London from her home village near Edinburgh—to enjoy herself? Hardly that; she was sent by her parents to look after her eldest brother, the black sheep of the family who was a perpetual source of anxiety. The girl, leaving home for the first time, was to act as a loving little dragon to this young man who was unable to keep out of debt. They saw none of the sights but spent long hours walking in the parks and exploring the old bookshops. The relationship between them was not strained by her mission, though she was a conscientious dragon. His debts were paid and she discovered a small outstanding one and decided that they must go without a midday meal till it was discharged. So to sustain them on their long walks they had only a bun apiece.

This episode was one of a recurring family pattern in which masculine weakness was accepted almost as a matter of course —Margaret's father had been a silent ineffectual man, her mother the sustaining and vital centre of the home, the two brothers were weaklings. Her own marriage repeated her mother's with variations. Frank Oliphant, her husband, was an unsuccessful artist with poor health. Had he been the wife instead of the husband, he could have reclined on a *chaise longue*, amusing himself gracefully with his designs for stained glass and eagerly admitting, nay proclaiming, his dependence on the breadwinner of the family who would have been free to devote himself to his task. As it was, poor Frank was made miserable by the fact that his wife earned more than he could ever command, even though interrupted by child-bearing and household duties. Immediately after the birth of the first child she is forced to write off to *Blackwood's*—"I cannot quite afford the luxury of keeping quiet." However, she was strong and hopeful and there was a short period of security when her husband's prospects seemed improving.

They had set up a home in London and she rejoiced in it and in her babies, for another followed quickly on the first. But every age has its own particular spectre and the consumptive haunts the nineteenth century: the fatal coughs of Mimi and Violetta on the operatic stage are as much period as their costume. Frank Oliphant's not very promising career was cut short by this all too common disease, in spite of a pitiful journey to Florence to find warmth in mid-winter. They travelled in unheated carriages, lost their luggage, and no one apparently had warned them that northern Italy could be desperately cold. Their lodgings were on the sunless side of the Via Maggio and were dark and damp. Such were the conditions which were to restore health to the invalid. Margaret used to go and look at the picture galleries for comfort but nothing cheered her husband. He would sit silent, crouched by the fire for hour upon hour. The glorious art treasures of Florence were to him only a mockery, the fermenting political excitement around them, which aroused his wife's keen interest and enthusiasm, seemed to him bitterly irrelevant. In the late summer his condition worsened. She nursed him night and day until the end, when she could report that he died "quite free from anxiety". He left her with two small children, an unborn baby, £1,000 of debt and a small insurance policy of about £200. Her second boy was born six weeks later and when asked how she was left, she replied: "With my head and my hands to provide for my children."

At thirty-one her married life was over but her husband had never at the best of times provided much support. She herself had certainly been an affectionate and self-sacrificing wife but in writing of Charlotte Brontë, whose passionate heroines she could not quite stomach, she says: "I have learned to feel that the love between men and women occupies in fact so small a portion of either existence or thought." That is not the remark of a fully satisfied wife.

She returned to England and settled in Scotland to grapple with her new life. At first everything seemed to go wrong—several articles for *Blackwood's* were refused and at last she proposed to embark on a serial story. The odds were against her. The august heads of the firm thought it would not be possible to take such a story, "though they were truly kind and sorry for me . . . I think I see their dark figures now against the light and myself taking leave of them as if it did not matter and so much afraid that they would see the tears in my eyes. I remember the walk down the hill and a horrible organ that played 'Charlie is my darling' and how one line of the song came into my mind— 'The wind was at his back.' The wind, alas! was not at my back, I reflected, but strong in my face both really and metaphorically." What follows is strikingly in character. After she had put the children to bed she sat down and began the story. She wrote for nearly the whole night. It was the first of *The Chronicles of Carlingford*, was accepted after all and laid the foundation of her success.

Slowly she built up her reputation as a writer and her security as a breadwinner. Then another fatal visit to Italy, this time as a holiday with friends, resulted in the death from fever of her little daughter Maggie, a companionable, bright and capable child. This was a terrible blow. Perhaps because anxiety and trouble were in her experience inseparably connected with the other sex, the mother had, as she admits, unconsciously been calculating more on Maggie than on any other hope in life. After wandering about Italy for a time, she settled down in Paris with her boys and continued the work upon which they all depended. It was during these sad months, curiously enough, that she wrote the light-hearted satire *Miss Marjoribanks* which wears better than the majority of her novels.

Finally, she settled at Eton so that her sons could attend the college as day boys. The proverbial Scots thrift was quite lacking in this family in which the women worked and spent and the men only spent. "I never too much thought for the morrow," she confesses. "I had always a conviction that I could make up for extra expense by a little exertion." A sense of pride and desire to spare her children made her unwisely hide from them the extent of the effort needed to earn the money that they spent so light-heartedly. A. C. Benson, who was a school contemporary of the elder boy, Cyril, remembers how she arranged everything for her son's pleasure and enjoyment, and in after years she wondered sadly if her easy ways had influenced this boy, who began life with so much promise and finished as yet another family failure. But at this period he was still the bright schoolboy and things went fairly smoothly with "the night-spinning spider" turning out book after book and articles on every conceivable subject. She was determined that, lacking a father, her children should not lack a mother too through the demands of her job, and the little house at Windsor was often filled with her sons' schoolboy friends. Private theatricals were held in the drawing-room and she wrote plays for them and sometimes acted herself. Something was always going on and the children's life was happy and carefree.

Fresh calls, however, were soon to be made upon her. Margaret's elder brother, William, had turned up at intervals, always a rolling stone, always in debt. Now her second brother failed in business and without a moment's hesitation she took his eldest child into her home while he went to make a new start abroad, but a year or so later a new blow fell which was to turn her already heavy responsibilities into an all but intolerable burden. Her sister-in-law died and her brother returned home with his two younger children and the whole family of five simply settled down to live with and on Margaret for the rest of their days. She describes him, a man of middle age, as leading a quiet life, reading his paper, taking his daily walk and sitting in his easy chair afterwards—showing a mild interest in his children and getting through life not unpleasurably. Apparently he thought it quite natural that his sister should maintain the whole family. She accepted it all with that matter-of-fact courage that made her a remarkable woman. It meant the end of her ambition to write as well as she could. She must now simply write as much as she could:

> "Of course I had to face a prospect considerably changed by this great addition to my family . . . I remember making a kind of pretence to myself that I had to think it over, to give up what hopes I had of doing now my very best, and to set myself steadily to make as much money as I could . . . but it had to be done and that was enough. One can't be two things and serve two masters. Which was God and which was Mammon in that individual case it would be hard to say, perhaps, for once in a way, Mammon, which meant the money which fed my flock, was in a kind of poor way God."

Although she firmly eschews any heroics over the sacrifice of her art and even asserts that it was probably not in her to produce a masterpiece, there are many indications that given less pressure the masterpiece might have been written. As it was, "there is too much of me for fame" she used to say ruefully but with truth. Pressure always with her resulted in prolixity and she had no competent critic at hand to tell her where and how much to prune. Her best work was always done in those rare periods when her family commitments eased a little. Meanwhile she comforted herself with this resolve: "If I can but rear three men who may be good for something in the world, I shall not have lived in vain."

Even this, however, was denied her. First, her nephew, a steady capable boy whom she had educated and then fitted out to take up an engineering post in India, died of typhoid after a year's promising work. She had relied on him for help with his sisters and sadly wrote of him: "Of all the family he was the one I was most secure about and had least anxiety for." Then Cyril, her elder son, who had had a brilliant career at Eton and a respectable one at Oxford, began to show signs of weakness and instability. His mother's high hopes for him steadily faded. She was continually helping him to start afresh. She wrote to Mr Blackwood once asking for his support in an application for a minor post in the Education Department: "He is not energetic but he would work in the routine of an office and he has plenty of faculty." Cyril died suddenly at thirty-four, having produced one little book on French literature, rather badly done, for a series his mother was editing. The younger boy, Frank, was more stable and worked hard at a qualifying exam for the British Museum which he passed with high marks but was rejected on the score of health. He settled down to desultory literary work and helped his mother with her travel books, by which means she contrived so that they might both winter abroad. This line was then something quite new, and her volumes on Florence, Venice and Jerusalem were justly popular.

She was sixty-two when the last of these commissions was undertaken and at sixty-two in the Victorian era one had entered old age. Moreover she suffered from feet badly crippled by rheumatism. Travelling was slow and uncomfortable; in Palestine it was by riding or walking only and accommodation was primitive. The journey then was no light undertaking, but she made little of fatigue, heat or other difficulties, not even of being pitched out of her palanquin on an expedition up Mount Carmel. Frank was a thoroughly congenial companion on all these journeys, but four years after the Palestine expedition he too died from heart failure and she was left alone except for the two nieces, who had never caused her any trouble or anxiety and who were now left as her only comfort. There was little need in the future for earning, but her work had become an overmastering habit and besides was, so she found, the only anodyne for grief.

Her last years were given to an exhaustive history of *Blackwood's* who had always stood by her and whom she had served so faithfully and well. It remains one of the most interesting accounts of a publishing firm on record. But now her hitherto splendid health began to show symptoms of cracking under the strain of lifelong overwork and many sorrows, and she welcomed the signs of the end. Her last article for *Blackwood's* was a masterly and spirited account of Queen Victoria's reign to mark the Diamond Jubilee. "'Tis Sixty Years" covers also the whole span of her own adult life and ranges with typical breadth of outlook over all the important changes that had taken place during the period. It ends with the statement: "There is nothing, as is well-established in history, that a woman does so well as to reign . . . in this she has ever held an uncontested place as high as the highest, needing no excuse on the grounds that she is 'only a woman'." This article was a fitting climax to the countless number that had flowed from her pen—all well-informed and readable. She knew herself to be near death, but with characteristic firmness she made up her mind to live till the Queen's Diamond Jubilee celebrations should be over. She had always had a great sense of an occasion and was determined not to let any nonsense about her death spoil the enjoyment of others on this great day. She did not want anyone to stay away from the procession on her account —"I promise you," she said, "you shall have no bad news." As always, she was true to her word—all the shouts had died away, all the splendour had faded, before two days later she died peacefully and happily, repeating to herself the names of her children.

Among the notices of her death, *The Times* hailed her "as one of the foremost women workers of the century" and *Blackwood's* affirmed that "Mrs Oliphant has been to the England of letters what the Queen has been to our country as a whole". The climate of opinion had modified slightly since Mrs Trollope was forced to maintain her family by her own exertions. It was accepted as less extraordinary that a woman should attain professional status, though it was made no less easy for them to be wife, mother and breadwinner all in one. Henry James wrote of Margaret Oliphant: "Her success had been in its day as great as her activity, yet it was always present to me that her singular gift was less recognised, or at any rate, less reflected, less reported upon than it deserved." But later, he added: "One of the interesting things in big persons is that they leave us plenty of questions and precisely one of those that Mrs Oliphant suggests is the wonder and mystery of a love of letters that could be so great without being greater." Had James been born a woman, and had he had a family of five children and one adult to maintain unaided, the question would have answered itself. The quality of work which Margaret Oliphant produced in such circumstances is so good that it is allowable to believe that with fewer cares she would have written better still.

As it is, she did much to benefit her generation at a time when the newly literate and leisured were hungry for education and she won for herself and for women generally the recognition that a wife and mother was capable of holding down a responsible professional job.

5
Married to an Archbishop

Mary Benson
1841-1918

Mary Sidgwick, at the age of eleven, an innocent and merry creature, was chosen by her masterful cousin, Edward Benson, to be his future wife. He sent her a love poem in which his sentiments were plainly expressed. Her parents, though they thought highly of the young man, then twenty-three, were naturally unwilling that their little daughter should be subjected to an emotional pressure unfitted for her age, and forbade further love-making.

But the future Headmaster of Wellington College, Bishop of Truro and Archbishop of Canterbury, was not even then an easy man to control. He was wont to ignore anything which stood between him and his strong self-confident and self-approved desires and he spoke to her of love again, kissing her hand and filling her with an oppressive sense of pride, unworthiness and guilt. He waited until she was just past her eighteenth birthday for marriage, but during those seven years left no doubt in hers, or anyone's, mind that she belonged to him. Her main preoccupation, poor child, was to become worthy of him and to please him, but as she grew older, with that honest self-analysis which was characteristic of her, she faced the fact that "though he had chosen her, she had not chosen him"; "I was happiest when I knew Edward to be happy and yet wasn't with him."

It was no accident that Edward Benson had selected a young malleable girl to be his bride. He was a born schoolmaster, full of energy and highly gifted, and he had a passion for creating beings in his own image. What chance had she against him? She wrote in the diary that was her secret companion and confidant:

> "An utter child, I danced and sang into matrimony with a loving but exacting, a believing and therefore an expectant spirit, twelve years older, much stronger, much more passionate, whom I did not really love."

Then she adds immediately, with her characteristic generous tolerance:

> "But let me try to realise how hard it was for Edward. He restrained his passionate nature for seven years and then got this unloving, weak, unstable child. I know how disappointing this must have been to him, how evidently disappointed he was."

Well, one is tempted to add, he was asking for it! If a man picks on a child of eleven he must be prepared to restrain his passion for some years and not take it out on her afterwards in "evident disappointment". Mary continues: "How hard for him, too, full of all religious and emotional thoughts and yearnings. They had never awoke in me."

He always believed that he could shape others to his own pattern, however different they might be in temperament or aptitude. They both did their best, he to mould, she to be moulded, but the first years of marriage were very difficult:

> "Certainly I did not vex Edward [by singing at a small dinner party] and I think that is as good a criterion as I need have."

84

"Edward said to me not long ago with such an earnest eager look and his eyes full of tears, 'Minnie, if you will only try, I will never be cross with you again.' I said, 'Are you sure?' 'Yes, sure,' he replied, 'but you must remember that your promise will be as hard to keep as mine.' God help me! I believe I shall persevere this time. If I can only stir up my apathy I can do a great deal."

It was not only that she was constitutionally unable to respond to either his physical or his spiritual ardours, she was also intellectually lacking in certain ways which he considered essential in one who was to be his life companion. She had a keen mind, praised in its time by Gladstone himself, but her children and her friends testify to the fact that she was singularly without any real interest in the arts or the sciences. Possibly the strain of having to please her learned lover and to satisfy his exacting standards stifled the natural appetite for knowledge in a bright, quick, but not academic girl. Edward's approval and not the mastery of a subject for its own sake was her aim and what he loved best was never what she would have chosen.

In the early days of their marriage, they took a trip abroad, greatly looked forward to by Minnie, but, alas, far from fulfilling its promise. To read of it in the great dutiful journal which she then kept is almost as painful as the account in *Middlemarch* of Dorothea's weary trip to Rome with Mr Casaubon. She begins, "I write this Diary in the hope that it may record an improvement in my life of which God knows there is only too much need." What follows is a meticulous account of all the churches, cathedrals, and abbeys they visited with such detailed architectural notes "that you would have thought", says her son, "she was qualifying for a clerkship in the firm of some ecclesiastical builder." From before breakfast sometimes till the close of day they carried out this specialised sightseeing for which Edward was passionately eager, but Mary cared not a rap. "I was so tired and knocked up that I could

85

not look at anything and what I did see I could scarcely remember," she confesses one day. Nevertheless that same evening, "I went to see a new church with Edward." She was at the time twenty-one, had already borne two sons and was carrying a third child.

Church architecture was dull, but accountancy was worse. "I have most woefully neglected my bills," she writes, "in spite of Edward's constant requests . . . the truth is I believe that I dreaded them. It is cowardly I know and now that I have done them I am going to give them to Edward this afternoon . . . What he will say I scarcely dare think . . . if we were alone, I could bear these hours better, but I have Mamma as witness . . . I know she takes my part and that makes it worse still . . . that confidence may be restored between us it seems as if I have to go through the Valley of the Shadow of Death." She did not actually bring herself to present these poor little bills for another two days.

"I must not think of being at ease," she confides to her private diary later, "but of suiting my ways to his feeling and this without a shadow of thinking that my ways are better than his, though I like them better." Thus she embraced her lot with a heroic abnegation of self which in a less strong personality would have resulted in negation and despair. With her it did not, because it was consciously willed. She found an outlet in friendship, confessing that it was here she first learned to love. In a fiercely literary and academic family she alone preferred people to books. It was the same with theology, politics and all the isms of the day. All that to her husband was of the utmost importance meant little to her, except as it affected him, and as he grew in influence and importance, so his claims on her, both private and public, grew also. In spite of all her efforts it was obvious to Mary that she was of those who had greatness thrust upon them.

"I really think that the spiritual or moral dilemmas of Mrs Jones, the curate's wife, interested her more than what Lord Salisbury said last night at dinner", said Ethel Smyth; and,

"Poor thing, she has no precedence", was the remark of a certain peeress.

Her approach to religion was also personal and fluid rather than doctrinaire and authoritarian. Once, accused of being a Dissenter, she replied: "By all means! if not caring two straws about the Apostolic Succession spells Dissent." But this was in later life. In her earlier years she kept her beliefs and her doubts to herself. For she did experience a period of doubt and distress and knew that Edward could not possibly understand or help. He was, though far more brilliant, a simpler person, quite alien to her questioning and analytical turn of mind. She finally won through to a faith which stood her in greater stead in the face of grief than her husband's unyielding dogmas. When their eldest son, an exceptionally promising boy, died at school, Edward was unable to accept the tragedy—in his eyes God, who he thought of as not unlike himself though Divine, a just, benign and powerful Ruler, had somehow committed an outrage. "Martin's death", he wrote very touchingly long afterwards, "remains an inexplicable grief—everyday. To see into that will be worth dying." To his wife, however, God was pre-eminently not the Divine Ruler but Divine Love, and her children were safe and fulfilled in that love even more in death than in life. "It is expedient that they go away", she quoted and believed, and she was, besides, so inured to self-sacrifice that her own loss appeared to matter little compared with their gain. Indeed, the toll that life took of her might be gauged from her general attitude to death: "You were in a net of knots and enmeshments from which there was but one release, since as long as you lived, you had to do your best with constraining circumstances."

Archbishop Benson was a passionately devoted father and husband but in each case his intensity of feeling came between him and the objects of his love. He longed for them to be perfect, fearing every small shadow that threatened their spiritual and moral welfare. "It was the sense of far-reaching momentous consequences", says his son Arthur, "which haunted my

87

father", and he tells as an example how, as a small boy, he started to take an interest in music and used to creep down to the piano early in the morning when he hoped to be undiscovered: "My father was working in his study—when was he not?—and I disturbed him. He looked in. He was pleased, I think, at my early rising, but I expect that a vision of my becoming a musical dilettante, and perhaps taking to the operatic stage, shaped itself before his vivid imagination. All he said was 'Hadn't you better read a useful book?' and my musical experiences were at an end, not to return for many years." Again, when Hugh, the youngest son, was falsely accused of bullying at Eton he says: "I was nearly paralysed in mind by the appalling atmosphere of my father's indignation and wholly failed to defend myself by tears of silent despair."

Such was the awe in which family and friends held Edward Benson that a word or frown of disapproval were terrible to bear and the young wife who had so early learned to dread his slightest displeasure realised later that she must act as a buffer between her children and this benign yet dreadful power. This situation was, of course, a common one in the Victorian family but Benson's dynamic and formidable personality made it the more stultifying and Mary Benson's tact and humour were hard-worked. The philosopher Henry Brewster, after a first encounter, put down the Archbishop as a "constitutional proselyter. How his wife's more fluid brain can accommodate itself to this temperament is obscure to me. She must suffer much."

And so the busy years went on—of devoted duty on her side and of enormous interest and success on his. It was typical that when at last the Archbishop's health showed signs of the unremitting strain to which he had subjected it throughout his career, he refused to admit the need of any slackening of pace. He was advised by his doctor to rest before and after meals during a strenuous tour in Ireland. His wife notes: "He is furious and won't." She was anxious and apprehensive but he, on the contrary, enjoyed himself enormously. On their return they went to stay with the Gladstones. Edward Benson sat up late talking, rose early, walked to early communion, walked again to matins and died quietly and instantaneously during the service.

The foundations of the family were shaken as if by an earthquake and they packed up and left England for the East to seek recovery from the shock. There, three of them were seriously ill. It is significant that Maggie, who was given up for lost, prayed aloud and ceaselessly, not to God, but to the Archbishop to make her well. Which, in the face of all the doctors' diagnoses, he did. Mrs Benson did not fall ill, but she was for a time utterly stunned by the blow. She was not overwhelmed by intense personal grief, the entries in her diary are very different from Queen Victoria's hopeless outburst after the Prince Consort's death. They are bewildered and groping. She was fifty-five and for almost as long as she could remember he had ruled her life. She was now a woman in late middle age who had to find herself. Was it too late? Her diary tells of her dilemma:

> "This ceasing of every stimulus, and this terrible inner sense that all my life, all these years, was derived from and in answer to distinct, never ceasing claims seems to kill me. There is nothing within, no power, no love, no desire, no initiative: he had it all and his life entirely dominated mine. Good Lord, give me a personality . . . Now all is over and nothing is required of me but to enjoy and that I can't do. I feel exactly like a string of beads, always on one string, worn, carried about till they seemed as if they had some real coherence. In a moment the string was cut.
>
> "The Vision of Personality . . . How to connect this with finding myself? I feel as if I had led a superficial life so long, not wilfully or wrongly exactly. But united as I was with so dominant a personality as Edward . . . combined with the tremendous claims of the position, how was I to find myself? . . . I seem only to have been a service of

respondings and no core. But there must be a core . . . I have never had time to be responsible for my life. In a way I feel more grown up now that I have ever felt before . . . for the first time I am answerable to nobody. No one has a right to question my actions and I can do as I like. What a tremendous choice."

In one sense it was too late, for the habit of selfless response to the needs of others was too strongly ingrained in her to leave her real freedom of choice. The mantle of Edward Benson had descended to some measure on his daughter Maggie who, after his death, seemed to develop many of her father's characteristics. She and her mother lived together in a home which was chosen because it suited Maggie and, in her mother's words, "gave her a sphere". The brothers came and went when they chose. In many ways the children were an anxiety and would have been a disappointment had Mary Benson allowed herself to think along such lines. Arthur refused the headmastership of Eton which she would dearly have liked him to have; he also suffered from periods of crippling depressive neurosis. Maggie was immersed in interests which her mother did not share and for the last nine years of her life was alienated by a tragic mental illness. Fred led the life of a successful society bachelor in London, and Hugh became a Roman Catholic priest. None of them seemed to have considered matrimony at any time and Hugh and Arthur definitely avoided women. Mrs Benson, as far as we know, made no comment, though so warm and selfless a mother may well have wished for grandchildren.*

Then there were all their books. These she read through as dutifully as she had once read up church architecture to please her husband, but with as little pleasure. Arthur's were too insipid, Fred's too worldly, Maggie's too scholarly and Hugh's were little more than propaganda. So that she surveyed

* The difficult marriage which begot this brilliant brood seemed in many ways to have produced a curious disharmony in their personalities. The different parts did not fit.

the ever increasing rows of volumes with an indulgent but rueful pride and on her eldest son's testimony, with one or two exceptions, they remained undisturbed. Mary Benson had herself suffered too much from direction and from "oppressive disappointment" when she had failed to come up to expectations not to let those she loved go free. Even when Hugh left the Anglican Church, which meant so much to her and of which his father had been the earthly Head, she could write thus: "You know well enough what a terrible blow any such step would be to me if I looked at it personally . . . But this is not the level on which I take it with my heart and will . . . I know your utter sincerity of heart and I only desire that knowledge and thought should come up to that—and I am not unmindful—dearest son, how *could* I be?—of all your pain and conflict and patience." And after his actual reception into the Roman Catholic community: "It seems as if the inner bond had got so much closer as the outer one has—what shall I say—changed?" Neither did her sense of humour desert her: "I have had a real prize of a letter from A.B. about you", she wrote to him. "She apparently hopes you are a little out of your mind. Such a simple way of accounting for it."

These letters on Hugh's defection are a striking example of the way in which, by deliberately putting herself and her own desires out of the picture, Mary Benson was able to sympathise with her children's very different choice as she had once subordinated herself to her husband's wishes. She never failed them in love and, what is more difficult, in trust. Even during the long years of Maggie's alienation her mother was able to keep before her the vision of her daughter's true personality as the reality behind and above the sad spirit which possessed her. What did develop as the core of personality for which she was seeking during her widowhood was an inner strength and a splendid zest for life. Her two great interests, people and religion, gained in depth and wisdom. Her clear analytical mind united to a warm heart, humour and common sense, made her invaluable to many who confided in her. She would have made a splendid psychiatrist.

The Benson marriage was an extreme example of the typical subjection of the Victorian wife to her husband's career and personality; extreme, because of the early age at which the process began and also because of the outstanding gifts of both the characters concerned. What was lost and what was gained by such a relationship? The loss to the wife was freedom. The prop provided was too strong and this plant was not of the clinging variety at all. Mary was undoubtedly forced away from her own natural development. She was deprived of the careless joy proper to youth and especially to her particular temperament. She suffered, too, perhaps a stifling of the love of knowledge for its own sake and both husband and wife might have found a more satisfying fulfilment with a different partner. But it was not by any means all loss. The flower of that firmly willed acceptance on her part was a deep affection and a strong growth of character. The plant was not in this case stunted; on the contrary it flourished, though always a little twisted away from its natural growth.

6
Married to a Mystic

Louisa Macdonald
1822-1902

Louisa Powell was one of a large, pious, prosperous, Nonconformist family. One sister was an active member of a society for converting Roman Catholics, the second sister spent her life in good works; theology was the staple diet of all. The eldest brother had married a beautiful Scots girl whose cousin, George Macdonald, had come to London to take up a tutorship in a friend's family. She brought him to the Powells and the effect was "as if a prophet had come amongst them". Louisa herself was away at the time but one of the sisters (there were six in all) wrote:

> "He will explain everything that puzzles you—he shewed me a new life in everything and understood me as an equal. This was very wonderful to me, as all my life I had been the fool of the family."

This remarkable young man, handsome and full of charm, was obviously ready to become someone's divinity, and pretty soon it became clear that Louisa Powell was the destined worshipper. But the phrase used by her sister is significant: "he understood me *as an equal*". This marks a fundamental difference between George Macdonald and our other Victorian male deities: though possibly the most fit, he is yet the least anxious to assume deification. "Believe, my dearest George, in the love of your most unworthy child", expresses Louisa's attitude correctly but the corresponding relationship is lacking on his side. The "little woman", "the sweet little wife", "the goody"— these infantile and condescending terms of endearment are all conspicuous by their absence in his love letters. She is from the beginning "Dear, dear Louisa", a person in her own right, and she responds by the most complete and open confidence, even about matters in which they differ, such as his far greater tolerance over doctrine. But all the more is she aware of unworthiness.

It was hard work sometimes to love and be loved on a basis of equality by one whose natural habitat was that country "far beyond the stars". Louisa even felt sometimes it would be better should they not marry. A habit of introspection encouraged by her upbringing did not help. She felt she did not love God enough to be the wife of such a man, also that she was too plain, too uninteresting and too irritable. Comparing herself with her sister-in-law, she exclaims, "How I wish I were as bewitching!" and again, "My heart is a strange one for fancying miseries and dreading the time when you will have got bored of me and I shall have no genius, no talent, no poetry, no beauty." To all of which George Macdonald answers, not by preachings, exhortations or teasing, but by building up her confidence in many small ways and in emphasising his growing reliance on her care for his health, which was poor: "I am sure I shall never be well until I have you with me always."

Mr Trollope's declaration of love was accompanied by a detailed statement of his financial position, Carlyle's by an outburst of black misery and an expectation of a life of suffering; George Macdonald's wedding present to Louisa was just as extraordinary to our way of thinking. It was a poem beginning cheerfully:

Love me, beloved, for thou mayest lie
Dead in my sight, 'neath the same blue sky.

This strange bridal song continues:

> Love me, beloved, for both must lie
> Under the earth and beneath the sky,
> The world be the same when we are gone,
> The leaves and the waters all sound on.
>
> Love me, beloved; for both must tread
> On the threshold of Hades, the house of the dead,
> When now but in thinkings strange we roam.
> We shall live and think and shall be at home.

These "thinkings strange", however, were familiar enough to George Macdonald all his life. He always held that "here we have no abiding home". His books are all concerned with a spiritual pilgrimage. It was no wonder then that he soon felt he did not fit into the narrow confines of the Nonconformist ministry as it then was. At first he fully intended to follow in the steps of his much loved father and was ordained and received a call to the Congregational Church at Arundel.

A severe illness postponed his marriage. The Macdonalds were all delicate, both his brothers died early of tuberculosis, and all their life together Louisa was anxious about George's health. She wished now to marry him immediately in order to nurse him but this was not considered proper by her family. On this occasion, as on many another, he showed no fear of death: "It is somewhat discouraging to be thus laid aside at the beginning, but the design of God in doing so will perhaps appear soon—or if not now, we shall know afterwards, and if never, it is well notwithstanding. There *is* a reason and I at least shall be the better for it." This faith upheld him always and his whole conduct of affairs was based upon it: "I do not myself believe in misfortune; anything to which men give the name is merely the shadow-side of a good." This attitude posed a more practical problem for Louisa than the lack of beauty or brains, for she had not his unquestioning faith and neither possessed common prudence. Their life together was a series of crises, financial and physical, which would have defeated most young couples.

Macdonald was soon banished from Arundel for his unorthodox opinions, among which was the hope that mercy might be shown to the heathen in an after world. This was shocking. The elders first docked his princely salary of £150 upon which he wrote to his father: "God has provided for us very lovingly. Our salary is reduced but not so much as we feared."

The next year, however, his position became untenable. There were now two babies to support but another letter says: "You must not be surprised if you hear that I am not what is called 'getting on' . . . I can hardly say I have any fear and but very little anxiety about the future. Does not Jesus say, 'Consider the lilies'." But the young mother confesses that she sometimes doubted whether God cared about them as much as he did the lilies.

They moved to Manchester, where Macdonald's aim was to hire a room and preach and teach the factory hands and all who wished to listen in return for what they could afford. He could at any time have obtained a chapel with a regular stipend but he would not again give up his freedom of thought and speech. He was completely without fear of poverty and there was plenty of this. An unexpected bill for £6, for instance, presented a serious problem. "It has done me real good, I think, for even in poverty like ours one is so much more ready to trust in what oneself has, than in what God had ready to give when needed." They found temporary lodgings, though both longed for a place of their own but "we may wait a little for a home here for all the Universe is ours—and all time and the very thought of God himself."

Marriage to a mystic may either rouse the ordinary mortal to a fury of exasperation, anxiety, frustrated prudence and even self-pity, or lift her up on to his own plane. Louisa's moods of doubt and suffering came nearly always when she was away from her husband for when together his sincerity and power carried conviction so that she could truly say to him: "I would rather be with you on starvation diet than anywhere without you but with all the luxuries of creation."

She certainly had need of courage. A first book of devotional poetry on which they had built many hopes was accepted but subsequently refused by a publisher: "I am thankful for the pleasure the expected publication gave me and so helped to keep my spirits up. Now I am able to let it go." Poverty drove them to accept hospitality from wealthy cousins, a great trial to Louisa. Their assured income was about ten shillings a week. Then George's illness struck again.

At length they were able to move into a house where they took a lodger and Macdonald managed to secure some lecturing which brought in about £30 a year. The lecturing in literature and physical science was for the ladies' college which Macdonald himself helped to found. Throughout his life he did much for women's education and though that of his own daughters was a sketchy and hazardous affair, yet that of his sons was little better. There was no sex discrimination in the Macdonald family; in fact the eldest boy, Greville, confessed that with three older sisters, a father and mother all feminists, he was early crushed by a sense of inferiority: "I even remember wondering how my mother could ever have married my father, he with all his merits being after all only a man!"

The long dramatic poem was at last published and favourably reviewed. It has little literary merit but is interesting psychologically. Louisa had felt that whereas her husband was "all heaven and earth to her", she to him was secondary to his love for God. In a word "he for God only" did not satisfy her though she fully accepted "she for God in him". He wanted to convince her that she was mistaken in her attitude. The hero of the poem first seeks God for the sake of his own soul and this is shown to be a kind of high selfishness. Finally he confesses that "less than all was too little to cast at the feet of his wife in whom God was present in his eyes." The poem helped to convince her and she could write: "Oh, this is my happiness—

to know that you love me so truly in spite of my plainness and ignorance and temper."

Another important outcome of the book was the friendship that later developed with Lady Byron, who was deeply impressed by it.

The hand-to-mouth existence at Manchester continued. After four years of marriage Macdonald paid a long desired visit to his old home in Aberdeen where his little sister was dying of tuberculosis. There was not enough money for Louisa to go too and the parting was painful. She does not hide her troubles: the children are ailing, the rude nursemaid broke their perambulator, a new one cost twenty-four shillings and when bought was too heavy for her to push. She begins to paint a table, which, when finished, is to be sold to her brother for £6. This table might have been a gold mine, the importance it appears to have for her and the burden it becomes. But after all, what else could a lady do in those days to earn money but paint tables? She is invited to stay with a prosperous married sister in Liverpool but the contrast of her luxurious living and her imagined patronage are hard to bear and Louisa only has fifteen shillings left in her purse: "It is the old story, if you were with me I should hardly see the darkness." She is forced to borrow £5 to pay the grocer but "I will work very hard at the Table. Ellen was here to-day. She looks so very well and plump and pretty and cheerful . . . it is all drained out of me . . . Ellen looks like a flower, I like a potato rind." On his side Macdonald had only four shillings in his pockets when he arrived in Scotland and after a month this had dwindled to two shillings and sixpence, but he has found her a perfect Scotch maid for £7 a year: "She can wash well, and make the children's clothes, do a room very well, cook, bake cakes, gets up well in the morning, is exceedingly good-tempered and very kind to children." Unlike the Carlyles' succession of maids, this really was a treasure and stayed with them a long while. Macdonald's father gave him £4 to take him and the maid home.

Back in Manchester the teaching and preaching to spinners,

weavers and mechanics continued, but everything was again brought to a standstill by another bad attack of lung trouble and he was ordered complete rest for six months.

> My harvest withers. Health, my means to live—
> All things seem rushing into the dark
> But the dark still is God.

Another child is born, the invaluable Victorian maiden aunt comes to the rescue, a purse is collected for the family, of £30 and an unknown admirer sends £20 and Macdonald writes to his father: "We are in no anxiety for a few months at least. I am ashamed to have written that last sentence—as if we should feel safe as long as we had means laid up in store!" But for Louisa, tired out with her pregnancy and with three small children, there were failures of faith:

> "I had been ill and my husband was still ill and we had nothing to do, and we did not know what would become of us. I knew it was all for the best as my husband was always telling me but my eyes were dim and my heart was troubled, and I could not feel sure that God cared."

Yet she shared to the full his splendid improvidence and it was at this period that she gave away the last sixpence in her purse to a beggar child. Now it was that Lady Byron came to the rescue. A sad, gentle but dignified woman, her benevolence lightened many a load among her friends and acquaintances. It was at her house that Henry Crabb Robinson*, the intimate of the Wordsworths and Lambs, first met George MacDonald, thus establishing a link between Regency days and a much later age, for Macdonald did not die till 1905: "Called on Lady Byron and found with her a very interesting man, a Mr Macdonald, author of a poem entitled 'Within and Without', which must read. The talk was altogether interesting."

* 1775–1867.

Lady Byron invited Louisa and George and the delicate little second daughter to Algiers for the winter, but it did not suit either Louisa or the child. However it gave them a much needed change of scene and introduced them to new and influential friends. Macdonald, unlike Louisa, had no sense of false pride. He believed in the work that God had sent him to do and that the workman was worthy of his hire, and Lady Byron met him on equal terms. "I hope it is no disgrace to me to be rich as it is none to you to be poor," she said. "If I can do anything for you you must understand, Mr Macdonald, it is rather for the public than yourself."

Manchester was now considered too dangerous a climate for bad lungs (one feels that this might have been thought about before) and Hastings was next settled upon for a home. They moved to the appropriately named Providence House, a commodious place of thirteen large rooms at a rent of £35 per annum and Macdonald, as before, hoped to scrape a living out of lecturing and writing. The first Christmas at Providence House is typical of the family's way of life. They had scarcely settled in, the furniture and books hardly unpacked, there were now five children under six, the second child was temporarily blind from ophthalmia caught in Algiers, but they added a homeless orphan to the five babies and invited in thirteen other poor children to share the Christmas tree, managing to provide a little gift for each.

After two years' struggle, George Macdonald was appointed Professor of English Literature at the newly established Bedford College for Women. He had made friends with Mrs Reid, the founder, with Frederick Denison Maurice, Dr Elizabeth Garett, Mrs Josephine Butler, and Madame Bodichon, all enthusiastic pioneers for women's education and rights. It is clear that Louisa's feelings of inadequacy owed nothing to her husband's attitude towards women. Indeed some of his friends thought he consulted her overmuch about his books. She could not always appreciate his most visionary writings and, more intelligent and less meek than William Blake's wife, would sometimes question them. She was, for instance, troubled over some of the symbolism of *Lillith*. But there is no evidence that this criticism did any harm. Letters between them are, on his side, written from a basis of complete equality, full of talk about his work, books, their children, and of course the faith which to him was life: "I have had a most strange and delightful feeling lately—when disgusted with my own selfishness—of just giving away the self to God—to be forgotten and grow clean without my smearing it all over with trying to wash out the spot. This evening I could relish nothing but a poem of Chaucer. We really have never surpassed him."

With George's appointment to Bedford College the family moved again to London; but the Professorship brought in very little, another son had been born, a book on which much labour had been spent was refused by publishers, Lady Byron had died and money was very scarce. It must be obvious by now that neither George nor Louisa were good managers. Sometimes there was not enough food and Lily, the eldest child, though only eight years old, realised the situation and, with five smaller creatures clamouring for their dinners, pretended she was not hungry. One winter afternoon of gloomy rain, Louisa had gone out to buy necessities with her last sovereign and had lost her purse. She returned to the house where the children were waiting. Darkness fell and Lily kept the family quiet while the mystic and his wife prayed quietly together in another room. Their silent "waiting upon God" was broken by the postman, who brought a letter from Lady Byron's executors enclosing a quite unexpected cheque for £300—a substantial sum in those days.

Macdonald's faith never failed though the struggle for an income continued. He was not a popular success as a writer though he had some devoted readers. Publishers fought shy of him and it was five years after the publication of *Phantastes* (1858), perhaps his best known book, that his first Scottish novel, *David Elginbrod*, was accepted through the good offices of Miss Muloch, the author of *John Halifax, Gentleman*. Louisa was always striving to live as he did from day to day without anxiety for the future but she found it very difficult, especially when he was away: "I am simply ashamed of having talked with you with all my insane changes of mood. They have been all true to me. But why have I troubled you with them? Because I have . . . felt as if what I felt was yours and interesting to you, especially when shut up with hideous thoughts, ugly truths and the Devil." One of the secrets of his power to subdue her doubts and miseries was that he did not condemn them: "Doubts are the messengers of the Living One to rouse the honest . . . Doubt must precede ever deeper assurance."

More fortunate than Mrs Benson who had to hide all her doubts away from the Archbishop, Louisa could turn to her husband secure in the knowledge that her honesty would be met with an equal integrity and imagination. And so often his childlike trust was justified. Money seemed to come like manna from heaven to pay outstanding bills or to provide for a holiday in Switzerland to bolster up Macdonald's frail health. It was only half enjoyed for Louisa, pregnant again, could not go with him. What seemed to give him most pleasure on this trip was climbing the towers of Antwerp and Strasburg cathedrals. All through his life stairways possessed for him an irresistible attraction. In each one of his fairy-tale books they constantly appear with symbolic significance. He writes now from the Continent: "I went up ill and came down well. Oh, my dear, what would you think of such climbing and such visions." An American lecture tour followed and this time Louisa left the children and braved the sea (she was an extremely bad sailor) and proved herself a perfect dragon in looking after her husband, sometimes cancelling long advertised lectures and refusing elaborate social entertainments when she thought his health would not stand the strain. Macdonald's business manager thought poorly of this odd client. "You make me sick!" he exclaimed, "yes, sick!" He was exasperated by his firm refusal to advertise himself and by his habit of preaching without a fee. Altogether the tour was not much of a success financially, in fact it was typical of the way these two babes in the wood of worldly wisdom managed their affairs. There were soon eleven children to be cared for—Macdonald said they had stopped on the wrong side of a dozen—but in a letter full of a new story he remarks casually, "I have about £8 in the bank and five in my pocket."

The children, of course, were accepted as gifts from God. The knowledge of birth control was unlikely to have reached such a couple and the practice of it was against all Macdonald's instincts, but it is not easy to measure how much a man is influenced by his times and he was no crank or doctrinaire, nor did he allow prejudice to close his mind to new ideas so that in the twentieth century his philosophy, while still resting upon his faith in God, might have allowed some modern modifications. As it was there were the eleven to be cared for but they were "serviceable children", according to one witness, "going about the house without troubling anyone", and what a house! Space and beauty are today such luxuries, especially in the vicinity of London, that we can hardly believe that this improvident pair could manage to take a great Georgian house in Hammersmith Mall with an acre of garden. Here at The Retreat — another symbolic name — collected writers, artists, musicians, actors, preachers, Christian Socialists with their train of poor protégées, all mingling together as if they were projections of the mystic's own dreams engaged in some fantastic dance. An Oxford graduate arrives begging, in rags, and stays for weeks, a drunkard in the process of being reformed comes with his lady love, a deserted consumptive wife, who took seven years to die and whose two small children (as if eleven were not enough) were adopted into the family, a little vagrant boy who is being trained as an organist, all are there, and in the garden with its tulip tree and walnuts and its statue of Artemis and quiet elm walk beside the Thames play the serviceable children while their elders drift to and fro in interminable talk.

Macdonald had no worldly ambition whatever for his children and, moreover, used to quote the fact that Hamlet was still at university when over thirty, so there was no hurry and anyway the children were learning how to care for others and much else. For sometimes all would combine in theatrical entertainments, dramatisations from French and English authors, songs and folk dancing to entertain a ragged audience. It was hard to tell where the fantasy world ended and the real world began.

For Louisa and her eldest daughter, Lily, the stage soon became the more vivid reality. Louisa seized upon it as a way of adding to the precarious and always insufficient family income. The production of babies was over and the production of plays took its place. Lily was found to have unusual dramatic gifts. The moral and spiritual aspect of such a scheme was satisfied by concentrating on a production of *The Pilgrim's Progress*, though Corneille and Shakespeare were also performed. For nearly ten years, performances by the family company took place in the summer all over England and Scotland, Louisa producing and designing the sets and costumes which were praised by Burne Jones, Lily acting the heroines, including Christiana, and George Macdonald himself taking the part of Greatheart and correcting the proofs of his books in the wings. There is no doubt that the performances reached a high professional standard but, like the famous painted table of earlier years, it is not at all clear that financially they were worth the enormous effort they demanded from the whole family. Greville Macdonald, less progressive than his parents, disliked his sisters appearing in public and thought it would injure their chances of marriage. He was justified in this for Lily's engagement was actually broken because she refused to give up her acting. But Louisa believed that these performances also made it possible for her husband to winter abroad and it is hard not to admire greatly the courage, talent and energy shown in carrying on such an unconventional activity through so many years. It is an oasis in middle-class Victorian conformity. Even two months after the death of Maurice, the youngest son, she continued undaunted. "I wonder whether you will be surprised to hear that we are intending to act our Bunyan's 'Pilgrim's Progress' wherever we can," she writes to a friend. "We have already made four engagements, the results of which will pay —and more—our journey back . . . The Pilgrim has become such a reality to us that it seems a *duty* to do it."

Some time before this The Retreat had been given up; its proximity to the Thames, like the damp and smoke of Manchester, was tardily considered bad for Macdonald's health. A gorgeous villa at Portofino (now the Hotel Splendide) was taken for a time and finally a great house at Bordighera, Casa Coraggio, was built in 1877 according to their own plans, including a living-room fifty-two feet by twenty-six with an organ. This was partly the gift (manna again) of loving admirers. It all seems fantastically inappropriate to the Macdonalds' means and way of life. But again one must remember the cheapness of living abroad and of labour, especially in Italy in the nineteenth century. Money troubles were never absent, however, though perhaps they should not be called troubles for they were not allowed to cause any real anxiety.

In 1885 Macdonald writes to his agent: "I don't know that ever I seemed worse off . . . I say seemed because I do not acknowledge the look of things . . . If I had a good offer for my house I would sell it . . . you see I have only one son off my hands yet. However they cause me no other burden whatever—thank God." Six years later a bank failure brought a substantial loss of savings about which Louisa says: "There is a nut for us to crack without any kernel. It doesn't seem very hard except for the children." But no money difficulties were allowed to interfere with the hospitality and music and reading and lectures and entertainments at Casa Coraggio:

> Please come on Monday,
> The day after Sunday,
> And mind you start with
> Something to part with;

A fire shall be ready
Glowing and steady
To receive and burn it
And never return it.

. . . .

We would not deceive you;
The fire shall relieve you,
The world will feel better
And so be you debtor.

George and Louisa Macdonald
Bonfire at 7 p.m.
Dancing at 8 p.m.

Other rubbish was burnt away at Casa Coraggio besides useless junk, prejudice and fear and narrow-minded exclusiveness. At Christmas in the great room there were *tableaux vivants* (a very popular Victorian form of drama) but these, inspired by Louisa's talent and knowledge, were really fine representations of medieval paintings and to them were invited the Italian poor children of the town to whom some of the English colony objected. Still more daring, a concert was actually given in aid of paying off the debt on the Catholic Church and this at a time when the anti-Catholic feeling in England was almost at its height. The Macdonalds were never afraid of unpopularity but there was no lack of appreciation among the Italian population and this was even greater after a severe earthquake in 1887 plunged the whole district into panic and poverty. Now Casa Coraggio proved a haven indeed: "We had one family to meals, their kitchen and roof having fallen in and another came to camp out in our big room for the night; but we had also to pack all the top storey into the ground floor. So an immense amount of packing, coaxing and a little manœuvring had to be exercised to keep our large household in good spirits and to keep off faints and hysterics." Louisa and her daughters managed to put courage and new heart into both visitors and townspeople and worked for weeks afterwards to help the stricken families. A second big shock followed while Louisa was sitting at the organ in the English church: "The whole building began to shudder, just like the skin of a horse determined to get rid of a gad fly." Her response was to pull out the stops and play the Hallelujah Chorus. George's attitude was even more characteristic: "It was worth having lived to know what power may be. You knew it must be none other than God. No lesser power could hold the earth like that, as if it were 'a very little thing'."

The earthquake left no sign of shock upon any member of the family. It was not earthquakes or money troubles but the loss of three of the much loved children which darkened, not their faith but their lives. The (to us) almost criminal lack of precautions and care of health, which through ignorance was common enough then, seems in the Macdonalds' case to have also partly resulted from the mystic's whole attitude to life and death; in life, his complete trust amounted to a sort of Christian fatalism, in death, to a denial of the usual significance of the word. In *Lilith* the most haunting and vivid scenes take place in the cemetery:

> " 'Are they not dead?' I asked softly.
> " 'I cannot answer you', the sexton replied. 'I almost forget what they mean by dead in the old world. If I said a person was dead, my wife would understand one thing, and you would imagine another.'
> ". . . 'But these are all dead and I am alive!' I objected shuddering.
> " 'Not much,' rejoined the sexton with a smile, 'not nearly enough! Blessed be the true life that the pauses between its throbs are *not* death!' "

And so when the eldest daughter, Lily, was dying, he could write to Louisa: "She has never taken care of herself and now we must take care of her" (but it was late for that!). "If Lily goes now, how much sooner you and I may find her again . . . We must remember that we are only in a sort of passing vision here, and that the real life lies beyond us." But the mother could not take the separation without anguish and looking back she felt bitter reproach:

> "But oh! Lily did suffer!—and indeed all her life she has been an intensely suffering soul. Knowing all I do now of what unintentional agonies we have made our children suffer, and all the while having a heart full of love and intended good will to them, I could not *dare* of my choice to have over again such a lovely family as was given us to rear and teach and guide."

It was a cry which could not be stifled and it implicated both, though one suspects that the father never felt like this, but the cry could be made to him none the less. Louisa had never hidden anything from him. Perhaps the memory haunted her of the child pretending not to be hungry when there was too little to eat because her husband would not compromise with his conscience. The children of idealists often suffer by being made to feel odd, by not being allowed to conform and in other less subtle ways, by actual neglect while their parents are busied with the claims of others. They may be made "serviceable" too often or too much considered as being like the lilies of the field or fowls of the air—able to flourish without earthly care. Yet the Macdonald children certainly had no reproach for their parents. They had from them the one thing needful: "the hearts full of love" and much besides. The "golden cock"* often crowed for them. There may have been poverty of material goods but there was no poverty of imagination or values. There was, too, respect for their personalities, a rare enough element in the Victorian family. "A parent must respect the spiritual person of his child", wrote their father in *The Seaboard Parish*, "and approach it with reverence, for that too looks the Father in the face and has an audience with Him into which no earthly parent can enter even if he dared to desire it." It is interesting

* *Lilith.*

to note that all the eight surviving children made happy marriages in after life.

The Victorian husband and father, too, often accepted without question the current assumption that he was a god to his wife and a hero to his children. George Macdonald who never wished to be either of these was in fact both—not in the least willingly. He disliked any form of hero worship, which seemed to him silly when all men and women fell so short of the true vision of reality, and the idea of man being superior to women seemed equally silly :

> "The one sex balances and rectifies the motions of the other. No one is good but God. No one holds the truth or can hold it in one and the same thought but God. Our human life is often at best but an oscillation between the extremes which together make the truth." [*The Seaboard Parish*]

George and Louisa Macdonald triumphed over many of the false ideas and assumptions which beset their contemporaries and came near to achieving that ideal equilibrium between husband and wife which is the highest achievement of marriage in any age.

7
Victorian Wives in Fiction

Dickens   George Eliot
Trollope   Mrs Gaskell
Thackeray   Miss Yonge
Meredith

The nineteenth century is the great age of the novel, and Dickens, Trollope, Thackeray and George Eliot, besides many a lesser writer, held a mirror up to the nature of Victorian society. Reflections in a mirror are sometimes brighter than the original, sometimes darker; but the whole effect is clearer and so it is often the mirror image which is imprinted on the mind. It is hard not to believe, for instance, that the popular concept of the Victorian female, heightened in its good and its evil, was not reinforced in the public imagination by the power of Charles Dickens's genius.

Throughout the crowded pages of his novels, we meet with three chief types of women—the witches, the angels, and the nitwits. Of these, far the largest group is the last; there are more thoroughly silly women in the work of Dickens than in that of any other novelist. The first group consists of fateful, sinister figures. They are closely connected with evil, sometimes of their own brewing, sometimes of others'; but even when guilty only by association these women do not escape the consequences of wrong-doing. They dwell in claustrophobic brooding worlds, each with its own particular horrors. Mrs Clennam in *Little Dorrit* sits always in her gloomy house surrounded by obscure rustlings and whisperings. Mrs Skewton in *Dombey and Son*, "with her false curls, and false eyebrows and showing her false teeth set off by her false complexion", is imprisoned in her bathchair and the mockeries of a wholly pretentious existence. At Chesney Wold, the home of Lady Dedlock in *Bleak House*, there is rain falling continually, like tears. Lady Dedlock is one of Dickens's fallen women. A realistic treatment of a very similar story is to be found in George Eliot's *Felix Holt*, but her Mrs Transome is a woman of flesh and blood with whom we can feel. We cannot feel with Lady Dedlock; we experience her as poetry and we are haunted by her as by a vision of despair. Storms, darkness, and mist are frequently associated with these lost souls who, like ghosts, fearing and feared, flee the frequented paths of ordinary society. They are the untouchables, between whom and the innocent and sheltered there yawns a tremendous chasm. Edith Dombey, even before she had run away, even though she had no motive but revenge, considered herself able to contaminate Florence by a touch, once she had decided to leave her husband: "Hurrying out, and up towards her room, Florence met her coming down". In reply to her outstretched arms, "Edith recoiled and shrieked. 'Don't come near me!' she cried. 'Keep away! . . . Don't speak to me! Don't look at me!—Florence!' shrinking back as Florence moved a step towards her, 'don't touch me!' "

Miss Havisham, the perpetual bride of *Great Expectations*, is another sinister figure. What does all the symbolism which surrounds her mean? The darkness: "She was shut away for ever from the daylight"; the death in life: "Without this arrest of everything, this standing still of all the pale decayed objects, not even the withered dress on the collapsed form could have looked so like grave clothes, or the long veil so like a shroud"; "the airless smell that was so oppressive", and "the speckled legged spiders with blotchy bodies" running ceaselessly in and out of the cobweb-covered wedding cake. The mirror image is reflecting something very odd and nasty here. Is it perhaps all that was morbid, self-regarding and self-destroying, claustrophobic, false and rotten in the Victorian attitude towards sex?

There are also other humbler and more squalid female creatures created by Dickens: Mrs Heep in *David Copperfield*, Mrs Squeers in *Nicholas Nickelby*, old Mrs Brown in *Dombey and Son*, reminiscent of some of the nastier witch hags of legend, inhabitants of the Victorian underworld of poverty and crime. Then the mirror reflections change from black to gleaming white. Dickens's heroines are all "angels in the house".

These angels, however, are not interesting. They share a common radiance which extinguishes individuality. We cannot learn much from them about young Victorian women because we cannot believe in the perfectly flawless goodness and purity of Florence Dombey, Little Dorrit, Esther Summerson, Agnes Whitfield and the rest. The significant thing is that these angelic beings were enormously popular and obviously satisfied the public and especially the male public taste. There is one exception to the angelic host. In Bella Wilfer from *Our Mutual Friend*, Dickens's last finished novel, he gives us a portrait of a good woman who has a few redeeming faults. Dickens seldom accompanies his heroines far into matrimony. As an arch romantic he found contemplation of a close day-to-day relationship between husband and wife unrewarding. He is fascinated always by the mystique of the unknown. The bride therefore is more attractive than the wife. The married women of Dickens's novels are made of very different stuff from his brides. This pseudo-romanticism about brides is not peculiar to Dickens, however; it was in the air. Anthony Trollope, who knew better, and who often refers to the truer sort of emotion which comes with knowledge and the shared years, has occasional lapses when he voices this bride-versus-wife cult:

"To know one is loved by a soft being who still hangs cowering from the eye of the world as though her love were all but illicit, can it be that a man is made happy when a state of anticipation such as this is brought to a close?"

Alas, the "soft being" who in youth captivated Arthur Clennam (in *Little Dorrit*), turned into the fat and foolish Flora Finch—a transformation that happened too frequently to Dickens's women. His unending gallery of fools is depressing; even allowing for the fact that neither his mother nor his wife was very sensible and that therefore he may have been more sensitive to stupidity in mothers and wives, the disproportionate numbers of silly females in the novels seems to point to a low standard of contemporary feminine mentality. But women who are not taught or even required to be sensible are seldom found to be so. Of course, Dickens accentuates their silliness. Still, we find it easier to believe in a Mrs Nickleby than in an Agnes Whitfield. Mrs Nickleby's stupidity corrupts her affection and is nearly the downfall of her poor daughter. As a character she is the epitome of all inconsequent senseless chattering females. Her brother-in-law is trying to persuade her that the calling of a milliner for Kate is an honourable and lucrative one:

" 'What your Uncle says is very true, Kate, my dear,' said Mrs Nickleby. 'I recollect when your poor papa and I came to town after we were married that a young lady brought me home a chip cottage-bonnet, with white and green trimming and green persian lining, in her own carriage, which drove up to the door full gallop;—at least I am not certain whether it was her own carriage or a hackney chariot, but I remember well that the horse dropped down dead as he was turning round and that your poor papa said he hadn't any corn for a fortnight.'
"This anecdote, so strikingly illustrative of the opulence of milliners, was not received with any great demonstration of feeling."

Mrs Nickleby is the doll-wife grown older but not wiser. Mrs Copperfield, Dora, Pet Meagles, and others of their type, over-protected and spoiled darlings, either meet with an early death or make unfortunate marriages or change into Flora Finches, Mrs Vardens or Mrs Nicklebys. Others, helpless and ignorant also, though not protected, meet with an even more disastrous fate. We see them grown old and pathetic, creeping through the pages of the novels, hiding from their horrid husbands—Mrs Quilp, Mercy Pecksniff and old Affery Flintwich:

> "Mistress Affery, by some means (it was not very difficult to guess, through the sharp arguments of her liege lord) had acquired such a lively conviction of the hazard of saying anything under any circumstances, that she had remained all this time in a corner . . . like a dumb woman.
> " 'Go before, you fool,' said Jeremiah (her husband). 'Go before, down, you Affery! and do it properly or I'll come rolling down the banisters and tumbling over you.'
> " 'Affery,' said Arthur, 'speak to me now!'
> " 'Don't touch me,' she said. 'Don't come near me! He'll see you, Jeremiah will. Ah, here he is. You'll get me killed!' "

From the victims in the gallery of fools we pass on to the tyrants, whose hard and narrow stupidity is even more unsavoury. These are those who exploit their affectations of frailty. The cult of the invalid wife is another unhealthy symptom of the current false sentimentality that surrounded women, which appears in more than one novel of the times. George Eliot's good-natured Mr and Mrs Pullet (in *The Mill on the* Floss), with their pride and pleasure in her multitudinous pills and potions, contrast rather forcibly with Dickens's none the less silly but also very unpleasant Witterlys from *Nicholas Nickleby*:

> " 'Mrs Witterly,' said her husband, 'is Sir Tumley

Snaffles' favourite patient. I believe I may venture to say that Mrs Witterly is the first person who took the new medicine which is supposed to have destroyed a family at Kensington Gravel Pits. I believe she was. If I am wrong, Julia my dear, you will correct me.'

" 'I believe I was,' said Mrs Witterly in a faint voice.

" 'Mrs Witterly is quite a martyr,' observed Pyke with a complimentary bow.

" 'I think I am,' said Mrs Witterly smiling."

Mrs Pullet hurts no one but herself by her silliness, but Mrs Witterly uses her invalidism to tyrannise over Kate.

" 'Don't talk to me [in that way], Miss Nickleby, if you please,' said Mrs Witterly, with a shrillness of tone quite surprising in so great an invalid. 'I will not be answered, Miss Nickleby. I am not accustomed to be answered, nor will I permit it for an instant' . . . Then she fell back upon the sofa, uttering dismal screams."

A number of most unpleasant widows are some of the worst tyrants among Dickens's characters. Too truly may Tony Weller warn his son Sam: "Beware of widders!" They have though the excuse that they existed in a world where the economic position of women was preposterously insecure. They had to make a living by fair means or foul, and Dickens saw to it that it was mostly foul! Breach of promise, child minding or baby farming, pretentious governessing, it did not matter what, they are all hard, ruthless and false :

"Mrs Pipchin's constitution was made of such hard metal, . . . a marvellously ill-favoured, ill-conditioned old lady, of a stooping figure, with a mottled face, like a bad marble, a hook nose, a hard grey eye that looked as though it might have been hammered at in an anvil without sustaining any injury . . . she was a great manager of children." [*Dombey and Son*]

"Mrs General's way of forming a mind was to prevent it from forming opinions. If her eyes had no expression it was probably because they had nothing to express. If she had wrinkles, it was because her mind had never traced its name or any other inscription on her face." [*Little Dorrit*]

There is this terrible vacuity among Dickens's women; even the normal and proper feminine emotions, devotion to husband and children, are made to look ridiculous because of the stupidity which accompanies them. Dear Mrs Micawber and Mrs Kenwigs are no less silly because they are harmless and good-hearted:

"Mrs Kenwigs was overpowered by the feelings of a mother, and fell upon the left shoulder of Mr Kenwigs dissolved into tears.

" 'They are so beautiful!' said Mrs Kenwigs sobbing. . . . 'I can-not help it, and it don't signify,' sobbed Mrs Kenwigs. 'Oh, they're too beautiful to live, much too beautiful!' " [*Nicholas Nickleby*]

Yet Dickens does not show much sympathy for any woman who tried to widen her horizons and take interest in matters outside her home. In the persons of Mrs Pardiggle and Mrs Jellaby they are mercilessly lampooned. Mrs Pardiggle is a social worker:

" 'Well, my friends,' she says to the bricklayers, 'I am here again, I told you you couldn't tire me, you know. I am fond of hard work and am true to my word . . . I am a School lady, I am a Visiting lady, I am a Reading lady, I

am a Distributing lady; I am on the local Linen Box Committee and many general Committees; and my canvassing
alone is very expensive." [*Bleak House*]

She was "a formidable style of lady with spectacles, a prominent nose, and a loud voice, who had the effect of wanting a
great deal of room", but her children are described as "dissatisfied and looking absolutely ferocious with discontent". Mrs
Jellaby, who works for the natives of Birrioboola, is the
mother of "poor sulky unhealthy Caddy" and of little Peepy
who fell downstairs. Mrs Jellaby on that occasion merely added,
with the serene composure with which she said everything,
"Go along, you naughty Peepy", and fixed her fine eyes on
Africa again. Mrs Pardiggle and Mrs Jellaby must have taken
quite a lot of living down, in fact their influence may still be
with us, Mrs Jellaby having become a synonym for those
women who work outside their homes and are thought to
neglect their families.

There are, of course, some sensible women to be met with
in Dickens, mostly among his out-and-out eccentrics or in the
respectable working classes, but they are few and far between
and one is left, after reading any one of the novels, with the
impression that he did not much like the women that he met
in the world around him and that in his phantasy world he left
them worse than he found them.

Anthony Trollope's novels offer perhaps the most reliable portrait of English middle-class society in mid-Victorian times. His
very limitations are an asset here. He is not passionately involved in his creations, he is too tolerant and genial a man
for anything but gentle satire. All intense emotion distorts, so
does too much cleverness, and Trollope never strains at reality
to prove a point. He was a man of the world, and a good mixer,
so that we feel he knew what a fair cross-section of the people
of his period were really like. We accept his characters as being

representative though they necessarily bear the hallmark of their creator.

His women especially are wonderfully convincing and they reflect, without distortion, contemporary attitudes and assumptions. They worship at the masculine shrine, they are seldom at all well educated, they are ignorant of sex, though, as we shall see, Trollope, unlike other Victorian writers, makes it clear that they experience it without knowledge. They are inescapably parasites, though the peculiar characteristics of Trollope's women is that they almost all possess the iron hand within the velvet glove. They are uncompromisingly firm, not to say obstinate, and often shown to be superior in morals, in sense and in judgement to the men whom they enthrone as their lords and masters. But although they are allowed to wield power in private and by strictly feminine means, woe betide them and all their circle if they attempt to interfere with the sphere of the real masters of destiny. The world of man, that is to say, the world of action, must remain inviolate or the natural order of the universe is reversed and chaos ensues.

Mrs Proudie, the wife of the meek and ineffectual little Bishop of Barchester, thinks she can run the diocese by direct intervention, with disastrous results. Vengeance descends upon her in the person of Mr Crawley, a poor and insignificant clergyman under a cloud for alleged theft, and yet a *man* with all a man's prerogatives. In an interview with the Bishop, at which Mrs Proudie insists on being present, he takes not the slightest notice of her frequent interjections until finally he turns upon her thus:

> " 'Peace, woman,' Mr Crawley said, addressing her at last. The Bishop jumped out of his chair at hearing the wife of his bosom called a woman. But he jumped rather in admiration than in anger.
>
> " 'Woman!' said Mrs Proudie rising to her feet.
>
> " 'Madam,' said Mr Crawley, 'you should not interfere in these matters. You simply debase your husband's high

office. The distaff were more fitting for you.' " [*The Last Chronicle of Barset*]

Mrs Proudie is one of Trollope's masterpieces. She is so real that her personality dominates the "Barchester" series of novels, and her death and not the clearance of Mr Crawley is the real crisis. She arouses about equal degrees of amusement, exasperation and finally pity. Trollope meant this pity to be for one who by her unwomanly behaviour ends by alienating and harming the husband whom she truly loved. But we can see Mrs Proudie's tragedy in relation to her times. In the modern world she would have found an outlet for her abilities in many useful ways—as chairman of committees, as a school manager, and a public speaker and even, if we take her a step further in time, as a bishop herself.

Lady Glencora, of the political novels, is a more complex character and her relations with her husband much more subtle, for she has great feminine charm but her meddling in man's world is none the less deplored and shown to be always unfortunate. When her husband, the Duke of Omnium, becomes Prime Minister, Lady Glencora is determined to make herself felt. She is shown to be injudicious, extravagant and all but dishonest, in spite of a good heart and good intentions, and quite incapable of understanding the finer points both of politics and her husband's character. She insists on backing a most undesirable candidate at an election, in direct opposition to the Duke's wishes:

> " 'You know how anxious I am,' he began, 'that you should share everything with me—even in politics. But in all things there must at last be one voice that shall be the ruling voice.'
> " 'And that is to be yours—of course !'
> " 'In such a matter as this, it must be.'
> " 'And, therefore, I like to do a little business of my own behind your back . . . You should let me have my own way

a little if you really believe I have your own interest at heart.'

". . . That he should be thwarted by her ate into his very heart;—and it was a wretched thing to him that he could not make her understand his feeling in this respect. If it were to go on he must throw up everything. Ruat coelum, fiat—proper subordination from his wife in regard to public matters. No wife had a fuller allowance of privilege, or more complete power in her hands, as to things fit for women's management. But it was intolerable to him that she should seek to interfere with him in matters of a public nature. And she was constantly doing so." [*The Prime Minister*]

The Duchess nearly succeeds in bringing dishonour on her husband and though she is sorry for his sufferings she is not really repentant:

" 'They should have made me Prime Minister, . . . I could have done all the dirty work . . . I could brazen out a job and I think I could make myself popular with my party . . . I could do a Mansion House dinner to a marvel.'

" 'I don't doubt that you could speak at all times, Lady Glen.'

" 'Oh, I do so wish that I had the opportunity,' said the Duchess."

Neither she nor Mrs Proudie had the opportunity and very troublesome they were both to themselves and to their poor husbands.

But any attempt in this direction is rare and for the most part Trollope's women, once they have enthroned their own particular Apollos and Jupiters, do not kick against the pricks. Examples of the maxim "she for God in him" are innumerable. Harry Clavering, even after having treated his Florence abominably, is welcomed back by her and her sister-in-law when he chooses to come "with one long ovation. He was, as it were, put upon a throne as a King who had returned from his conquest and those two women did him honour, almost kneeling at his feet." Frank Greystock had behaved to Lucy Morris even worse but was received into the Fawn household again with acclamation:

> "Nothing was now too good for him. An unmarried man who is willing to sacrifice himself is, in feminine eyes, always worthy of ribbons and a chaplet . . . and though he desired neither to eat nor drink at that hour, something special had been cooked for him, and a special bottle of wine had been brought out of the cellar. All his sins were forgiven him. No pledge or guarantee was demanded of the future. No single question was asked as to his gross misconduct during the last six months."

Again (in *The Way We Live Now*) after Paul Montague's intrigue with the American, Henrietta Carbury proudly asserts: "They should all know her heart was unchanged."

Poor dear Mrs Crawley, with her impossibly difficult husband (whose failings, though not his virtues, had much in common with Mr Trollope, senior), is forced to refuse proffered help in spite of a half starved family. "I can do nothing", she said, "but what he bids me"—"Wifelike she desired to worship him and that he should know that she worshipped him." Mary Lowther writes triumphantly to Janet Fenwick: " 'I have a Jupiter of my own now' . . . She was without a doubt, the man was her master and had her in his keeping and of course she would obey him." Mary Thorne welcomes back her lover: "There he was, Frank Gresham himself, standing there in her immediate presence, beautiful as Apollo."

But these god-like creatures are by no means always wholly estimable in character and moreover their worshippers know this and it makes not a scrap of difference to them. Here Trollope clearly recognises sexual attraction to be as strong for the woman as for the man—an astonishing admission for a Victorian, veiled though it is. A man such as Mr Gilmore (*The Vicar of Bullhampton*), or Roger Carbury (*The Way We Live Now*), or John Eames (*Small House at Allington*), may have all the honest worth, the reliability, the worldly goods, the sheer niceness of character, the patient devotion, which should ensure a response from any sensible parasitical female, yet their Lillies and Marys and Lucys and Henriettas prefer the handsome flaunting faithless ones, and why? "It was not at all delicate perhaps but the fact nevertheless remained. She had never felt herself disposed to play with Mr Gilmore's hair, to lean against his shoulder, to be touched with his fingers" (*The Vicar of Bullhampton*).

A painful and interestingly clear case of sexual repulsion, on the other hand, occurs in *The Eustace Diamonds*. Lucinda Roanoke, urged repeatedly by her aunt (to whom she owed her living) to marry Sir Griffin Tewett, succumbs at last but finds herself quite unable to master her repugnance to doing so. At the first kiss after they became engaged:

> "She did not revolt or attempt to struggle with him but the hot blood flew over her entire face, and her lips were very cold to his and she almost trembled in his grasp . . . When she was alone she stood before her glass looking at herself and then she burst into tears. Never before had she been thus polluted . . . The embrace had disgusted her . . . And if this, the beginning of it, were so bad, how was she to drink the cup to the bitter dregs?"

She found she could not. The day before the marriage her lover tried to coax her to sit on his lap:

> "She had acknowledged that she was bound to submit to be kissed. He had kissed her, and then had striven to drag her on his knee. She had resisted—violently."

After Sir Griffin had left her, Lucinda tells her aunt that she cannot go through with the wedding:

> " 'When he touches me my whole body is in agony. To be kissed by him is madness.'
>
> "The horror which the bride expressed was, as Mrs Carbuncle well knew, no mock feeling, no pretence at antipathy . . . But had not other girls done the same thing, and lived through it all and become fat, indifferent and fond of the world? . . . Of course the marriage must go on; though doubtless, this cup was very bitter. It had been her own doing and Sir Griffin was not worse than other men."

But Lucinda is as firm as all Trollope's young women and the marriage did *not* take place.

This incident, for it is scarcely more (Lucinda is not a main character), has a significance out of proportion to its part in the plot for it is perhaps unique in Victorian fiction in revealing without disguise the physical degradation undergone by many a poor young victim of the marriage market. Dickens and Thackeray do not attempt to be so explicit.

But let us consider those happier brides who love to caress and to be caressed by their lovers. They do not, in their innocence, hesitate to consign quite happily these same heroes to an unlimited period of waiting for the consummation of marriage:

> "Florence had made up her mind that she would be in no hurry. Harry was in a hurry, but that was a matter of course. It would be better that they should wait, even if it were for five or six years. She had no fear of poverty for herself but it was her duty to think of the mode of life that will suit him. 'It will do him good to wait,' said Florence." [*The Claverings*]

128

A strict code operates among Trollope's heroines that once the admission of love is made, even though it be to themselves alone, they hold themselves sacredly bound to their Apollos. They may be deserted, or circumstances may render marriage impossible—it makes no difference to their almost holy vows of lifelong devotion. No equal pledge was ever demanded from the hero. This situation occurs again and again and one heroine may speak for them all—Rachel Ray's hero, Luke Rowan, disappears under a cloud of suspicion and popular opinion runs high against him, but Rachel never wavers, though they have met only four times.

> " 'Didn't I tell him that I would love him . . . and I do love him, with all my heart and all my strength and nothing that anybody can say can make any difference. If he owed ever so much money I should love him the same. If he had killed Mr Tappett it wouldn't make any difference.' "

Marriage is openly acknowledged by Trollope as "a woman's career . . . and though there may be word-rebellion here and there, women learn the truth early in their lives. . . . Girls, too, now acknowledge aloud that they have learned the lesson; and Saturday Reviewers and others blame them for their lack of modesty in doing so—most unreasonably" (*The Vicar of Bullhampton*). Even those few women in the novels who are of independent means, such as Miss Mackenzie and Miss Dunstable, are shown as eventually seeking matrimony, if only in self-defence : "Without the hope of marriage she could be but a thing broken—a fragment of humanity created for use, but never to be used." Those women who have lost their husbands and have no children are poor creatures indeed, they have no occupation and no interests. The boredom, the emptiness of the lives of Lady Ongar and her like can hardly be imagined today and yet the descriptions of such lives carry a dreary conviction. Any man who fancied himself as a likely Apollo had no such scruples in forcing his attentions on any woman with means. No shame attached to a husband who lived on his wife's income, in fact of course there was no such thing as a wife's legal income, all her property on marriage being automatically her husband's. She was held to be fully recompensed by the status of a wife. On the other hand, if a man of substance married a relatively poor girl, even though she might be his superior in every other way, he was regarded, and often regarded himself, as something of a hero.

In discussing the possibility of Major Grantly's offer to Grace Crawley : "It can hardly be that a man is bound to do a thing, the doing of which, as you confess, would be almost more than noble." True, Grace's father was under a shadow of theft as well as being poor but no one really thought that he was a thief and Major Grantly had loved her before the accusation. Everyone, however, including the Major himself, and above all Grace, simply couldn't get over his nobility.

The financial aspect of marriage bulks largely in Trollope's books. He was a practical and materialistically inclined man who had suffered from improvident parents. It is noticeable that although devotion is nearly always shown as stronger in women than in men, it is more often they who are the ones who refuse to enter upon matrimony without sufficient means. They are aware that a man must be maintained in the luxury to which he has been accustomed : "Frank, I am so far selfish that I cannot bear to abandon the idea of your love. But I am not so far selfish as to wish to possess it at the expense of your comfort" (*Ayala's Angel*). The main problem of a Victorian marriage between such a middle-class couple is today less central but then it was one which was absolutely vital. It is stated unequivocally more than once by this realist, here again in *Ayala's Angel* : "If two people marry they are likely, according to the laws of nature, to have very soon more than two. In the process of a dozen years they may not improbably become ever so many more than two . . . With the cradles must arrive the means of buying the cradles."

But given sufficient income, Trollope is happy to follow their fortunes beyond the church door. This makes him particularly interesting for our purpose, for, unlike Dickens and Thackeray, he gives us many pictures of good seasoned marriages and of the relationship between middle-aged husbands and wives. These are usually good. If a woman is unhappily married, Trollope sees that the scales are heavily weighted against her, but, unless the man is utterly hateful, as was Sir Hugh Clavering, the wife is shown as adapting herself fairly success-fully to adverse circumstances. Unsatisfactory couples are the exception in the novels. The separate spheres of husband and wife were so well defined and so universally accepted that, as between the different classes in a feudal society, there is more ease and security than in a freer and more fluid community, so there was often a comfortable clarity in a Victorian mar-riage. A wife knew what was expected of her and, if wise enough never to venture outside her allotted sphere, was able to remain mistress of most situations that she might encoun-ter. As marriage was held to be the fulfilment of woman's exist-ence, in most cases it became so. Trollope gives us, in nearly every one of his novels, examples of the ordinary affectionate day-to-day relationship between couples who trust and esteem one another and co-operate fully in the job of living: the Grantlys, the Wortles, the Fenwicks, the Robarts, the Burtons, the Chiltons—the list is impressive. The husband is still of course the lord and master, the Jupiter whose word is law. But that word may be judiciously tempered or even altered by the wise wife who knows when to speak and when to hold her tongue.

" 'You would have made a great deal worse job of it than I have done,' said Archdeacon Grantly. 'I don't say you have made a bad job of it, my dear, but it is past eight and you must be terribly in want of your dinner.' "

Trollope liked women and his women characters are on the

whole a remarkably likeable lot. He recognises that life is harder for them than for men because they must put all their eggs into the one basket of matrimony. He does not for a moment think that this can be helped, nor even that it should be so, but he does allow them to enjoy the married state and to function usefully within it. There is not a dolly wife, nor a frustrated bitter young Florence Nightingale amongst them. There are parasites but no vampires and there is only one adventuress, Lady Eustace, who is harmless indeed compared with Thackeray's Becky Sharpe. Even the not quite respectable, but wholly irresistible Madeleine Neroni, the lovely cat among the plump pigeons of the Close, has a great sense of humour, a good temper and a kind heart.

Trollope was in no sense a feminist but he recognised and accepted women as individuals and was at least as interested in them as in men. That he thought them, in general, to be less worldly, more unselfish and endowed with greater powers of patience and endurance is partly to be explained by the fact that, in common with his contemporaries, he believed that it was both right and inevitable that women should be sheltered from the rough and tumble of the world and should devote themselves to their families. But that he also often gave them stronger characters and firmer wills than their husbands is probably due to his own peculiar home circumstances and the respective personalities of his father and mother.

Trollope, under the influence of the prevailing fashion rather than that of his own better judgement, praised Thackeray's silly little doll wife, Amelia Osborne, but any of his own heroines, though they might well have married handsome, worthless George Osborne, would have made a much better job of it than she did. Trollope's wives manage to adore their husbands without losing their self-respect. Thackeray never allows his "good" women dignity. If they are not dissolving in tears, or fainting away in somebody's arms, they are raging in some jealous and uncontrolled passion. Yet we are expected to admire them, or are we? Thackeray's attitude towards them is curiously twisted. Dickens at least liked and believed in his "angels" even if he does not make *us* do so, but Thackeray shows up *his* angels as often silly, coy, jealous, selfish, possessive and dishonest, while insisting at the same time that they are sainted beings. The one exception is Ethel Newcome, but she does not qualify for sainthood in the accepted idealistic Victorian sense. She is at first undeniably worldly and vain: "I, who rail and scorn flatterers—oh, I like admiration! I am pleased when the women hate me and the young men leave them for me." It takes a family catastrophe to elevate her, at the end of the book, into the true position of heroine.

The truth is that Dickens and Trollope were quite happy as Victorians, whereas Thackeray always seems like a man upon whom the Victorian mantle sits uneasily. It is perhaps not an accident that he sites three out of five of his novels in a preceding age, but he cannot escape the influence of his environment and all his "good" women characters bear the imprint of that Victorian society which he consciously or subconsciously dislikes. Many times Thackeray voices, either directly or in the characters nearest to his own views and experiences, a generalisation about women, good-natured enough, but none the less disparaging:

> "The Ladies, Heaven bless them! are, as a general rule coquettes from babyhood upwards."

> "The book of female logic is blotted all over with tears."

> "All women are jealous."

> "Well! What hypocrites women are!"

> "A perfectly honest woman, what a monster would such a female be."

These amiable traits of coquettishness, emotionalism, jealousy, and dishonesty are illustrated copiously by his heroines. Amelia is perpetually resorting to tears, Laura Pendennis is dreadfully coy and arch, Ethel is a coquette, Theo Warrington can be hypocritical but, worst of all, Rachel Castlewood and Helen Pendennis, who are constantly held before us as the perfection of womanhood, are guilty of venomous jealousy and the cruelty born therefrom.

Honesty and humour are only allowed to his "bad" women. Becky Sharp and Lady Castlewood can take a joke even against themselves and are capable of self-knowledge, but Helen Pendennis and Lady Castlewood do not admit their real motives either to themselves or to anyone else. "I am not good, Harry," says Beatrix, "my mother is gentle and good like an angel. I wonder how she should have had such a child." Yet this mother, as soon as she sees that her sixteen-year-old daughter has captivated Harry, proceeds to blacken that daughter's character to him under the guise of a sanctimonious warning. One of the first things, indeed, that we are told about Lady Castlewood is that "as soon as she had to do with any pretty woman she became cold and retiring and haughty". Helen Pendennis views Laura solely in the light of a wife for her son, chosen because, bound as Laura is by ties of gratitude and dependence to herself, she could count on her continued adoration and servitude. When Laura actually has the spirit to refuse Pen's filial proposal, Helen who, of course, has been prying and peeping on the couple unobserved from behind a window, turns on the poor devoted girl with the utmost fury. Again, when Pen becomes involved with humble little Fanny, his mother, always immediately thinking the worst of everyone concerned, including her son, arrives at his lodging, where his life has actually been saved by Fanny's nursing:

" 'I—I wrote to you yesterday, if you please, ma'am,' Fanny said, trembling in every limb as she spoke.
" 'Did you, madam?' Mrs Pendennis said. 'I suppose I

may now relieve you from nursing my son. I am his mother
you understand.'

" 'He does not know me, ma'am,' Fanny said.

" 'Indeed. Perhaps he will know his mother. Let me pass
if you please.' "

She had not a word of thanks or of kindness for Fanny, says
Thackeray.

Mrs Pendennis is later discovered at Pen's bedside: "She had
her Bible on her lap without which she never travelled." Her
first movement after seeing her son had been to take Fanny's
shawl and bonnet, which were on the drawers, and bring them
out and drop them down upon his study table! She drives Fanny
away from him and subsequently intercepts her pitiful little
letters. The virtuous Laura is just as unpleasant on this occasion and just as unjustifiably suspicious of Pen: "He had been
guilty and with *that* creature." When it is eventually proved
that Pen had not seduced Fanny after all but only broken her
heart, Helen actually collapses from joy, for there doesn't seem
any other reason for her sudden death:

" 'He's innocent, thank God! Thank God!' . . .

" 'Yes, dearest Mother,' he said. 'I am innocent, and my
dear Mother has done me a wrong.'

" 'Oh, yes, my child, I have wronged you—thank God.
I have wronged you!' Helen whispered. A little time after
Laura heard Pen's voice calling from within . . . She rushed
into the room instantly and found the young man, still on
his knees and holding his mother's hand. Pen looked round,
scared with a ghastly terror.

" 'Help, Laura, help!' he said, 'she is fainted—she's—' "

Laura, it need hardly be added, "screamed and fell by the side
of Helen. The sainted woman was dead." And the reader, at
least, breathes a sigh of relief.

Did Thackeray ever ask himself why he found it impossible

to portray his "good" wives and mothers without harping on their jealousy and possessiveness and smothering affections? He was obviously troubled by defects in the upbringing of girls: "A young man begins the world with some aspirations, at least he will try to be good and follow the truth . . . but by long cramping and careful process a girl's little natural heart has been squeezed up." She has been taught to be mercenary from her cradle; or again, "the prudery of our females is such that, before all expressions of feeling, or natural kindness and regard, a woman is taught to think of herself and the proprietaries." So with Laura Pendennis who, involuntarily, has stretched out a hand in sympathy to Warrington, "modesty checked, as of course it ought, spontaneous motion", and: "Kindly friendship shrank back ashamed of itself." But he did not clearly trace the more subtle faults of his heroines to their roots. A quotation from John Stuart Mill might have helped him here:

> "An active and energetic mind, if denied liberty, will seek for power: refused the command of itself, it *will* assert its personality by attempting to control others. To allow any human being no existence of their own but what depends on others is giving far too high a premium on bending others to their purposes."

Thackeray reproduces these conditions for his women with convincing fidelity and so, whereas Dickens's heroines are too good to be true, Thackeray's are too true to be good.

The interwoven pattern of dolls, slaves and tyrants is ruthlessly exposed in Thackeray's novels. Amelia is shown to be exasperatingly stupid and wilfully blind and it is to the "bad" woman we must go if we want to hear the refreshing truth: "You are no more fit to live in the world than a baby in arms. You must have a husband, you fool." To pave the way for this Becky proceeds to demolish Amelia's adolescent fixation on George: " 'Look then, you fool,' Becky said, still with provoking good-humour, 'you know his handwriting. He wrote that to me—wanted me to run away with him—gave it to me under your nose, the day before he was shot and served him right.' "

Rosie MacKenzie in *The Newcomes*—"Pretty little pink faced Rosie, in a sweet little morning cap and ribbons, her pretty little fingers twinkling with a score of rings, simpering before her silver tea urn which reflected her pretty little pink baby face"—is even stupider and a great deal more shallow and useless than Amelia, whilst her mother is "seeking for power" with a vengeance: "Rosie sat under Mrs MacKenzie as a bird before a boa constrictor—doomed, fluttering, fascinated, scared and fawning as a whipped spaniel before a keeper."

So much for dolls and tyrants, and as for slavery—"I was thinking that all women were slaves one way or another," said Ethel Newcome sadly, and indeed it is hard to find one of Thackeray's heroines who was not so.

> " 'Get a friend, Sir,' says Barry Lyndon, 'and that friend a woman, a good household drudge who loves you. That is the most precious sort of friendship, for the expense of it is all on the woman's side. The *man* need not contribute anything. If he's a rogue, she'll vow he's an angel, if he's a brute she will like him all the better for his ill treatment of her. They like it, Sir, these women. They are born to be our greatest comforts and conveniences.' "
>
> [*Barry Lyndon*]

Before becoming slaves to their husbands and sons, the likelihood was that wives had been slaves to their parents and victims, many of them, to the demands of the mercenary marriage market. Thackeray makes unequivocal use of the word "sold" in this connection. Ethel Newcome is in the process of being "sold" by her ambitious old grandmother and her impecunious father and is only saved by the desperate condition of her sister-in-law, "sold", in her turn, to the detestable Barnes. Poor Clara is driven by his cold-hearted tyranny into the arms of her faithful lover and runs away with him. The terrific scandal which follows frees Ethel from her engagement to a title and fortune, and brings her to her senses. Although Thackeray does not surround the dishonoured wife with quite such an aura of melodramatic horror as Dickens would have done, yet pure but pitiful little Laura Pendennis is vouchsafed a dream which she relates to the wretched Clara:

> " 'My dear, I dreamed that a bad spirit came and tore [your children] from you and drove you out into the darkness, and I saw you wandering about and looking back into the garden where the children were playing. And you asked and implored to see them and the Keeper at the Gate said, "No, never!" And then—then I thought they passed by you and they did not know you.' "

But Laura's dream was of no avail. It is significant that, although Barnes was an ogre and Jack Highgate a warm true-hearted man who had loved Clara and been loved by her before her marriage and faithfully ever since, yet he and she were doomed to a life of misery and exile together. Clear as it may be where Thackeray's sympathies lay, it was more than could be expected of any Victorian writer to allow a runaway couple any happiness. The institution of marriage was too sacred for such violation in the name of love. But Ethel was saved to become the only bearable "good" heroine in Thackeray's novels and to marry the hero Clive, mercifully released from his poor pink little Rosie who, although they were penniless and estranged, was yet "always in a delicate situation". One miscarriage too many and Clive was left free for Ethel, who, we may hope, retained enough of her original Thackerian badness to keep her spirited and honest and unpossessive, in a society where such attributes for wives were difficult to acquire and maintain.

So far, we have only explored the Victorian wife from without, in the fiction of men novelists; now we will look at the picture from within, as revealed by women themselves. George Eliot, the foremost woman writer of this period, in the portraits of Maggie Tulliver and Dorothea Casaubon, gives a painfully vivid study of the frustration and heartache so often suffered by the highly intelligent and sensitive woman while, in Rosamund Lacey, she shows how a narrow upbringing and lack of education can ruin more lives than one.

What appeared both proper and permanent in the role of a wife to the male novelist of the period was beginning to be questioned by women writers, for among the intelligent and thoughtful there had been stirrings ever since Mary Wollstonecraft, "that hyena in petticoats", as Horace Walpole called her, had published her *Vindication*. The Victorian woman novelist then, herself a portent, felt called upon to define and discuss the whole question of women in society, whether or no she approved of any change and, as novelist readers were predominantly women, she was thus instrumental in making them self-conscious about their rights and duties. The time was not ripe for any real development, it was only as yet an uncomfortable troubling of the waters. Mrs Gaskell, writing to her friend Eliza Fox, confessed that she sometimes wished "that we were back in the darkness where obedience was the only seen duty of women". Whatever they wished, women writers are distinguished from men novelists by their preoccupation with this question as well as by their innate sympathy and understanding for the wife who is now seen from within.

George Eliot's standpoint was a unique one. As a writer she extolled all the Christian virtues, yet acknowledged that she did not belong to any Christian denomination. She upheld the highest standards of morality, yet her extra-marital relationship with George Lewis exiled her from the most correct circles of society. She was emotionally extremely feminine in that she always craved for masculine support, yet she possessed an intellect which reached far beyond the education and opportunities allotted to her as a woman. No wonder, then, that she was peculiarly fitted to understand both the rebel and the conformist and to trace the reaction upon them of their environment. First, those who were nearest to her own character: she saw that the lot of such sensitive, thoughtful, aspiring beings was often unhappy, but she believed that it was also often inescapable. "A woman can hardly ever choose, she is dependent on what happens to her . . . she must take meaner things [than a man] because meaner things are within her reach," says Esther in *Felix Holt* (1866). If she is lucky she will find fulfilment in furthering the work and well-being of a husband worthy of her devotion, as Esther did. If she is unlucky and also unwise (but how is wisdom to be learnt by these intellectual waifs and strays?) she, like Dorothea Casaubon, or Gwendolyn Harleth, or Janet Dempster, will suffer a tragic frustration which can only be redeemed by serving others.

At the very end of *Middlemarch* (1871–2), perhaps the greatest novel ever written upon the theme of marriage, George Eliot speaks out in her own person:

"Among the many remarks passed upon Dorothea's mistakes, it was never said in the neighbourhood of Middlemarch that such mistakes could not have happened if the society into which she was born had not smiled on propositions of marriage from a sickly man to a girl less than half his own age—on modes of education which make a woman's knowledge another name for motley ignorance —on rules of conduct which are in flat contradiction with its own loudly-asserted beliefs. For there is no creature whose inward being is so strong that it is not greatly determined by what lies outside it."

Dorothea, "with her yearnings after large yet definite duties" and her hopes of identifying herself with the grand masculine scholarship of Mr Casaubon for the good of humanity, is nearest to her creator's heart, with the sad story of her first marriage, but this is only one of a quartet of young couples whose destinies are interwoven in the small provincial town of Middlemarch. No less disastrous than the Casaubon alliance is that between the clever young doctor Lydgate and beautiful selfish Rosamund Vincy. Lydgate with his brilliant potential is placed in direct contrast to the useless pedant Casaubon, and Rosamund with her fashionable accomplishments and narrow social ambitions to Dorothea's idealism and unconventionality. Rosamund ruins her husband's life but we see that she also is a victim of her environment. No one either at home or at school has provided her with a true sense of values and, even more than Dorothea, she is denied any real fulfilment. This is reserved for the other two wives. First, on a lower plane, Dorothea's sister Celia provides an example of someone who is by nature entirely content with those meaner things of which Esther talked. As the wife of the cheerful commonplace but kind baronet, Sir James, whom Dorothea despised, she is as comfortable and pretty and wholly satisfactory as a cat on a cushion. She takes what she wants with no fuss and no fumbling and, as what she wants is both biologically and socially acceptable, everyone is happy.

Mary Garth, the fourth young wife, is one of those women to whom George Eliot brings unqualified approval. They are not so dear to her as the visionaries but they make better wives, especially Victorian ones: "A man is seldom ashamed of feeling that he cannot love a woman so well when he sees a certain greatness in her nature—having intended greatness for men." Mary Garth and her kind have none of this uncomfortable quality. They are strong yet tender, homely yet intelligent, practical yet sympathetic. They are occasionally sharp-tongued but they are also quick-witted and humorous. They are too clear-sighted to make any bad mistakes and at their best have a true and deep wisdom. They are all country women and seem to have something elemental and enduring about them. They keep a clean hearth, a bright fire, an ordered household and welcome home happy husbands. Of such are Dolly Winthrop and Nancy Lammeter in *Silas Marner*, Mrs Poyser in *Adam Bede*, Mrs Garth, Mary's mother and Mary herself. They fulfil perfectly the highest function which George Eliot sees practical for the women of her day and age, that of being the presiding deity of the home, entering the man's world only at second-hand but supreme in her own, and therefore feeling herself on equal terms with her husband. Mary Garth marries Fred Vincy, Rosamund's brother. He has had a better chance of acquiring sound values than his sister, first through the wider experience which was his by right of his sex, and secondly through his boyhood's friendship with the whole Garth family, so that he determines, just in time, to follow his true bent for farming in the teeth of his family's misplaced ambitions. Fred Vincy and Mary therefore achieved a solid mutual happiness. Fred used to say of the Vicar, who had also wished to marry Mary : "He was ten times worthier of you than I was." "To be sure he was," Mary answered, "and for that reason he could do better without me. But you—I shudder to think what you would have been—a curate in debt for horse hire and cambric pocket handkerchiefs."

There is one other couple in *Middlemarch* important to George Eliot's conception of marriage. But they are neither young nor attractive and the husband is both a coward and a fraud. The wife is a typically respectable, rather showy, middle-class housewife. It has suddenly been revealed to her that her husband whom she has always revered and trusted has been deceiving her and all Middlemarch society, that he has been detected in dishonesty and is openly disgraced before all her relatives and friends: "Mrs Bulstrode's honest ostentatious nature made the sharing of a merited dishonour as bitter as it could be to any mortal." After the disclosure she goes to her room and shuts herself away to come to terms with it. In a passage of classic simplicity George Eliot lifts this very commonplace woman on to a different plane from any that we could have apprehended for her, where with dignity and pathos she meets and masters her fate as a wife. For "the man whose property she had shared through nearly half a life and who had unvaryingly cherished her—now that punishment had befallen him, it was not possible for her in any sense to forsake him . . . She knew, when she locked her door that she should unlock it ready to go down to her unhappy husband and espouse his sorrow and say of his guilt, I will mourn and not reproach." At last she does go to him :

> "He dared not look up at her . . . and as she went towards him she thought he looked smaller—he seemed so withered and shrunken. A movement of new compassion and old tenderness went through her like a great wave and putting one hand on his . . . she said, 'Look up, Nicholas.'
>
> "He raised his eyes with a little start and looked at her half amazed for a moment; her pale face, her changed mourning dress, the trembling about her mouth, all said 'I know', and her hands and eyes rested gently on him. He burst out crying and they cried together, she sitting at his side. They could not yet speak to each other of the shame which she was bearing with him, or of the acts which had brought it down on them. His confession was silent and her promise of faithfulness was silent."

A faithful loyalty in marriage was more frequently demanded from the Victorian wife than from the husband. Society exalted the family and the linchpin of the family was a reliable and dutiful wife. George Eliot regarded faithfulness as pre-eminently important, preferably on both sides but unquestionably for the woman. The ability to forgive generously is recognised as an essential virtue in all her heroines, even when great wrongs are involved, such as Janet Dempster (in *Scenes from Clerical Life*) suffered. Janet is driven out of her home by a cruel and drunken husband but returns to nurse him lovingly in her last illness.

Other women novelists also accept this point of view, however much their sympathies are involved with the wives. Mrs Gaskell's Silvia (*Silvia's Lovers*) discovers that her husband has tricked her into marriage by allowing her to believe that the man she really loved was dead. When he appears again and claims her, she curses her husband but will not break her marriage vows to go away with the man she loves and to whom she was first promised. Moreover she lives to repent the curses on her husband as a sin against God and man.

Mrs Gaskell breaks new ground with her novels about working-class wives, whose dependence and submissiveness towards their husbands were even more marked than in the middle class. "A woman should obey her husband and not go her own gait. I never leave the house wi'out telling father and getting his leave . . ." says Silvia's mother, although she knew very well she was "her man's" superior. She was a woman "whose only want of practical wisdom consisted in taking him for her husband".

Again in *Lizzie Leigh*, James Leigh and his wife Bell had been married for twenty years:

> "For nineteen of these years their life had been as calm and happy as the most perfect uprightness on the one side and the most complete confidence and loving submission on the other could make it. Milton's famous lines might have been framed and hung up as the rule of their married life, for he was truly the interpreter, who stood between God and her; she would have considered herself wicked if she had ever dared even to think him austere, though as certainly as he was an upright man, so surely was he hard, stern and inflexible."

Bell's first and last rebellion came over the erring daughter, Lizzie, whom the father had cast out. The wife had then felt bitterly against her husband "as against a tyrant"; and, of course, like very many Victorian family men, he was indeed a tyrant. She became sullen and resentful but the habit of submission was too strong to allow her to speak out. Trollope deals with exactly the same situation as a subsidiary theme in his *Vicar of Bullhampton* and perhaps it is significant that he shows his meek old Mrs Brattle as fearing and loving her tyrant too greatly even to harbour resentment. Mrs Gaskell as a woman feels strongly for her wives and mothers and with the erring daughters, too, though she never says outright, "This should not be." She devotes another whole book, *Ruth*, to a compassionate presentation of the fallen woman theme and touches on it also in *Mary Barton* and she was attacked for this. However, as in *Lizzie Leigh*, it is often the mother-child relationship rather than the marital one that seems to interest Mrs Gaskell most. She herself was a dutiful wife, but a devoted mother. In an age when there was often no real bond of shared interests or responsibility in marriage and when the sex relationship was so frequently doomed from the start, when therefore husband and wife were held together mainly by social and economic necessity and by an accepted code of behaviour, both often sought in their children the companionship and the emotional satisfaction they had missed in each other.

In her two best novels, *North and South* and *Wives and Daughters*, Mrs Gaskell, probably unconsciously, lays the real emphasis on two pairs of mothers and sons and fathers and daughters. In *North and South* the love motif between hero and heroine has a symbolic rather than a human interest. That is reserved for Mrs Thornton and her passionate absorption in her son John and, to a lesser degree, for Margaret's relationship with her father. In *Wives and Daughters*, Mr Gibson's feeling for Molly and Mrs Hamley's for Osborne, "that beautiful, brilliant young man", his mother's hero, are stronger than any conventional love interest. Indeed, Mr Gibson's and Molly's absorption in one another, their jealousy and sensitiveness, would have delighted Freud. The married couples were ill-matched, the extrovert, hearty country squire with his delicate, romantic wife, and the honest Dr Gibson with his selfish insincere little harpy. He is the typically blind and obstinate male who misunderstands his daughter, his stepdaughter and the supremely silly woman whom he marries in order to give his supremely sensible daughter the protection she does not need. He chooses for this role the pretty, genteel governess whose ignorance is only matched by her cupidity. She is as foolish as one of Dickens's wives but drawn with far greater subtlety. The evil effects of Mrs Nickleby's stupidity upon the fortunes of her daughter, for instance, are all objective; those of Mrs Gibson upon her daughter, Cynthia, are upon her character and whole outlook on life. Mrs Gibson's excuse is again to be found in the financial straits of widowhood, for which she is no match, and she wraps herself within such a cloud of pretence that she is no longer capable of understanding truth. The Gibson misalliance could have occurred in any age but such dismal failures were more likely in one in which false ideas of gentility, exaggerated prudery and the financial dependence of gentlewomen darkened and confused understanding between the sexes.

A widespread influence pervading mid- and late-nineteenth-century homes was that of Charlotte M. Yonge's multitudinous books. A lesser figure in the literary world than either George Eliot or Mrs Gaskell, because of this very fact and also because of her enormously larger output, she probably appealed to a wider feminine audience. She too was of irreproachable respectability. But her impact would have been nothing like so great had she not possessed the power of creating characters in the round. Her canvas, apart from her historical romances, is a narrow one, confined in fact to the upper middle-class family, but within this limit there is infinite variety. Among her pages the ordinary Victorian woman found fast friends, who were experiencing life as they themselves knew it. There is the intelligent eager girl, the young and often perplexed wife, the patient filial daughter or daughter-in-law, the harassed mother, the experienced matron and the lonely widow. These, however, are no types or symbolic figures but individuals, existing in their own right and to each and all Charlotte Yonge speaks with no uncertain voice.

In place of the veiled criticism of Mrs Gaskell and the resignation of George Eliot to women's lot, she brings a fervour of acceptance. The doctrine of women's subordination is embraced with ardour and provided with a moral and religious sanction: "I believe as entirely as any other truth which has been from the beginning that women were created to be a helpmeet to man." Her weakness and inferior status she affirms is a punishment for the transgression of Eve, "and that there is this inequality there is no reasonable doubt . . . womankind in general is still Christian enough to accept her lot and though often thinking of her obedience lightly, she knows by general example, even if she have no deeper thoughts, that her husband must be master and that hers must be the second place. If her thoughts are deep they go to the great mystery of which marriage is the type:

> Showing how best the soul may cling
> To her celestial Spouse and King.
> How He should rule and she with meek desire approve."

Here, Charlotte Yonge's view concurs with Coventry Patmore's contemporary doctrine, but coming from a woman it is less offensive and especially as her wives manage to retain their dignity while yet fulfilling their high calling as the helpmeet of man. To be cowed by timidity in fact is one of the ways in which a wife may fail and the difference between true meekness and the slave mentality is often stressed. Patient Griseldas must achieve gentleness and not have it thrust upon them. Still less, through an assumed weakness either physical or mental, should they become a deadweight on their husbands. There is plenty of real invalidism among women in Charlotte Yonge's books, as there was in reality. Margaret May is bedridden after an accident, Violet Martindale in *Heartsease* is frail and exhausted by too early pregnancies ("I shall be so glad to be seven-

147

teen. I shall feel as if baby would respect me more"), Cherry Underwood has a tubercular hip. But all these struggle against their disabilities. The selfishness that resorts to invalidism in order to obtain its own way (also a fairly common phenomenon as we have seen from other novels) is roundly condemned.

There is a third and more positive way in which a woman may fail to achieve the role for which she was created. She may rebel. These are women with strong wills and quick minds. For women's minds are quick rather than deep, Miss Yonge reminds us, as poor dear Ethel May found when she tried to keep up with her brother Norman in the classics. She could get so far but no farther, not even with the help of her father's spectacles and Norman's books, in the intervals she managed to snatch from her feminine tasks and duties. But, though perverse, these wayward ones are often the most promising as helpmeets and many of Miss Yonge's most interesting characters belong to this class of highly intelligent, but only youthfully rebellious, young women—for they are all reformed in time. True, we do meet with one or two thoroughly unattractive older women of the *maîtresse femme* type but they are never allowed to get away with it. No mercy would have been shown to Trollope's Lady Glencora. Even to organise a charity bazaar might be the beginning of the end, and the end was always bad and sad. How could it be otherwise considering that to trespass in any degree upon the man's world was to stray from the divine decree? But, when tamed, the masterful girl often becomes the noble wife. Here are a few of them.

Rachel Curtis (*The Clever Woman of the Family*), like George Eliot's Dorothea, prayed only "for action and usefulness" but found, again like Dorothea, that this was easier desired than accomplished and instead does much harm until she is finally rescued from her misused self by the strong, wise male, Captain Aleck Keith, v.c.

Theodora Martindale in *Heartsease* (1854), equally clever and self-willed, nearly wrecks several destinies but luckily falls in love with Percy Fotheringham, explorer, who is strong enough

148

to cope: "That home thrust at her pride, astonishing as it was that anyone should venture it, and the submission that followed had been a positive relief [to her]." Later, however, she defies her Percy, of course with disastrous consequences, but she repents before it is too late: "I was unbearable. No man of sense or spirit could be expected to endure such treatment. But I have been very unhappy about it, and I do hope I am tamer at last, if you will try me again." And her brother Arthur gives his blessing: "Such a pair is not to be found in a hurry. You only wanted breaking-in to be first-rate, and now you have done it."

Then, there is Wilmet Underwood (*Pillars of the House*). She could hardly escape a managing disposition, poor dear, having been left in joint charge with her brother of eleven younger children. (Could, in any other period, an indigent father on his death-bed be made to exclaim in eager thanksgiving on receiving the news that his delicate wife had just had twins: "My full twelve and one over, and on the Twelfth Day.") Wilmet met the challenge gallantly, but there is a subtle hardening of character not quite befitting, which has to be dealt with before she can qualify as the perfect helpmeet. At the first clash of wills after her marriage with Major John Harewood: "There was no temper in her tone, only the calm and reasonable determination that had governed her household and ruled her scholars." But later the inevitable retribution followed. Things went wrong and then Wilmet remembered, "He had commanded and she had disobeyed." She did not need to learn the lesson twice.

One more clever self-willed girl, Janet Brownlow, in *Magnum Bonum*, is punished far more severely. She had had the audacity to suppose that she, instead of one of her brothers, could complete her late father's medical discovery. When she finds, as of course she must, that this is beyond her powers, she has the ill luck and bad judgement to entrust herself and her secret to an impostor. She is finally redeemed but allowed no happiness. This severe treatment is due not only to the temerity of her ambition but also to her lack of candour and of filial obedience which Charlotte Yonge rates as highly as that of a wife towards a husband.

All these strong-minded women have in common the lack of parental authority and all of them seek out masterful men for their husbands. Charlotte Yonge's psychology was seldom at fault.

Dickens's and Thackeray's "angels in the house" sicken us, Coventry Patmore's evoke pity, only Miss Yonge's bewitch us into believing, while we are under their spell, that all was well with the Victorian doctrine of the perfect helpmeet, for only she, among all our novelists, possessed the rare gift for making that peculiar blend of angelic goodness attractive and convincing. Her born helpmeets are gentle and sweet and yet delightful, they are both intelligent and lovable, and the best of them, Violet Martindale in *Heartsease* and Christina in *The Dove in the Eagle's Nest*, are full of character. Christina, though in correct fifteenth-century setting, is as Victorian as the rest in her attitude towards her husband.

Charlotte Yonge was no sentimentalist. She believed in couples knowing each other well and loving each other in spite of faults and failings. But, living when she did, she was a romanticist and anyone such as Flora May or Alda Underwood who takes a husband for any other reason but love is ruthlessly dealt with, though however great the punishment there is no question where their duty still lies. The love match however is shown to be capable of standing up to both outward and inward stress and of creative growth, often through the spiritual ascendancy of the wife. For if woman is Eve, and therefore culpable and inferior, she is also Mary, Queen of Heaven. Though no one believed more heartily in the subjection of women than Miss Yonge, this was always in earthly and not in spiritual matters. Women are not only allowed but encouraged to call their *souls* their own and so they retain their dignity in spite of all the meek obedience demanded of them. It so falls out then that in her stories Milton's maxim "she for God in him" is often paradoxically reversed.

All in all, it was probably the case that the Victorian girl nurtured on Charlotte Yonge had as good a chance as any of finding happiness in that state of life to which it had pleased God to call her.

George Meredith's rebellious strong-minded clever heroines, Clara Middleton, Diana, Aminta, could not have existed earlier in the Victorian novel but, born of a new vision stirring abroad, they in turn reinforced and enlarged that vision. Meredith, whose own first marriage was a failure, saw that much of the tragedy in what he calls "one of the primary battles of the world, that between men and women" was due to wrong social patterns from childhood. "Bring up boys and girls together", he writes in *Lord Ormont and his Aminta* (1894), "they're foreigners when they meet. Teach men and women to be one, for if they're not, then each is a morsel for the other to prey on." His advanced views were probably due to the sort of education he had himself received, not at the regulation English public school but at a co-educational school in Switzerland kept by Moravian Brothers, where he imbibed ideals of tolerance and justice.

His most accomplished and popular novel, *The Egoist*, is closely related to his essay *The Idea of Comedy*, where he stresses the fact that the true comic spirit, by which he means a divine balance between emotion and reason, the individual and society, cannot exist where there is not a basis of equality of status between the sexes. Clara Middleton, the heroine of *The Egoist* finds herself, a young and, needless to say, ignorant girl, wooed impetuously by a wealthy, handsome, proud and universally admired suitor, Sir Willoughby Patterne. Her mother is dead and her father, a self-indulgent, indolent scholar, is strongly in favour of the match. She agrees, but discovers quite soon that Sir Willoughby is the complete egoist whom she can neither esteem nor love and towards whom indeed she feels a growing aversion both mentally and physically. The latter is not ignored or slurred over as it would have been by Dickens or Thackeray. The "clash of a sharp physical thought" at the idea of the intimacy to be incurred by marriage brings a sense of horror to Clara almost from the first and she takes every opportunity of avoiding Sir Willoughby's caresses. The whole of the book is concerned with her struggles to free herself from her engagement. The fact that this is so difficult is due not only to Sir Willoughby's character but also to her father. Filial obligation and parental power in disposing of a daughter was still strong. Mr Middleton dismisses his daughter's cry for help as foolish, her plea of dislike for the marriage as simply a feminine whim, and he is greatly influenced in this opinion by the fine quality of his prospective son-in-law's port. Besides she must marry someone—"a husband was her proper custodian, justly relieving a father"—and who more suitable than Sir Willoughby Patterne? Clara's realisation of her father's selfish inadequacy increases her misery: "She asked herself what her value was if she stood bereft of respect for her father." To disown an engagement which father, fiancé and her social circle considered binding would apparently bring such guilt and contempt upon the poor girl (and we may infer upon any poor girl) as to mark her for life. If Willoughby refused to let her go, only disgrace of one kind or another can be her lot. What then of this monster himself? His name is worth noting: he is a Patterne, and Meredith evidently meant him to be no extraordinary or unique figure but the epitome of an English gentleman of good breeding who possessed all the "manly" virtues. When cornered by a conscience-stricken friend with, "Own up, you have drawn Sir Willoughby Patterne from me," Meredith answered, "No, no, my dear fellow, I've taken him from all of us, but principally from myself." Sir Willoughby is, of course, a figure of high comedy and, as such, a pure distillation of egotism, yet Meredith certainly meant him to hold a mirror up to his contemporaries.

As then, the pattern of the upper-class Victorian male image, he conforms to many a hero both in fact and in fiction. He wished his bride to come to him "out of cloistral purity", to be like "fresh gathered fruit in a basket". He demanded "the sensual satisfaction of perfect bloom". "Applied to Sir Willoughby", says his creator, "as to thousands of civilised males the touchstone [of love] found him requiring to be dealt with by his betrothed as an original savage . . . To keep him in awe and hold him enchained, there are things she must never do, dare never say, must not think." Clara, speaking to Willoughby's earlier cast-off lady love, that "faded violet", Laetitia Dale, exclaims: "Has it never struck you that very few women are able to be straightforwardly sincere in their speech, however much they may desire to be?" The pattern husband, having secured his empty-minded but cloistral mate, will next proceed to exact the necessary worship from her. The Egoist is always chary of the world, fearing a jolt to his self-love. A woman of the world, Mrs Mountstuart, describes him to Clara: "The secret of him is that he aims at perfection, and I think he ought to be supported in his conceit of having attained it, for the more men of that class, the greater our influence, as men don't comprehend his fineness, he comes to us; and his wife must manage him by that key. You look down on the idea of managing. It has to be done."

Clara's lack of love is not important. Far more serious is her avowal: "I can endeavour to respect. I cannot venerate him."

At the last she is only freed by the sacrifice of Laetitia Dale on the altar of Willoughby's vanity. He realises that his "faded violet" is after all more to his purpose than the inexplicably wrong-headed Clara. Laetitia gives in simply through lack of money to support her own failing health and her invalid father. This explicit insistence on the importance to women of financial independence and its rarity is a new note struck by Meredith with penetrating realism. It is the underlying theme of *Diana of the Crossways*. Diana herself is modelled on the character and life of Mrs Norton, Sheridan's grand-daughter and the heroine of a *cause célèbre*, whom Meredith had met. Diana, like her originator, was beautiful, an authoress, unhappy in her marriage, and involved in a political scandal. Meredith says he had to endow his fictional character with brains unpossessed by Mrs Norton. This is hardly fair. Naturally she did not sparkle with Meredith's particular type of wit like Diana, but actually she was an abler woman and would not have made Diana's errors. She had children and it was for them and through them that she chiefly suffered and she broke out of the narrow circle of her own wrongs to champion the cause of all oppressed wives. Diana on the other hand was absorbed only in herself, but one of the points Meredith stresses about her is that her failings and her troubles largely arose from her want of money. Possessed of financial independence, she would not have made a rash marriage, would have been able to write her novels in comfort, would not have courted popularity by parties for which she had no means of paying and above all, would not have treacherously sold a political secret confided to her by her lover. Her sense of inferiority towards him —"an adventuress, who was a denounced wife, a wretched author, and on the verge of bankruptcy"—drives her to her doom. Ironically, in order to surmount this inferiority, she yields to the mad temptation of gaining monetary equality by betraying his confidence: "She had a secret worth thousands! . . . she began to tremble as a lightning-flash made visible her fortunes recovered, disgrace averted, hours of peace for composition stretching before her."

But she is adrift in a man's world and her dream of equality is hopeless.

A simpler, braver and luckier heroine succeeds Diana. Aminta married Lord Ormont, an Army officer, years older than herself, whom she has revered as a hero. He is, however, a disgruntled fellow who is embittered because he thinks his merits as a soldier have not been sufficiently recognised. Aminta becomes disillusioned with her god and realises too that her worship is not a mature relationship between man and wife. Lord Ormont is not so repulsively egoistic as Sir Willoughby, but he nevertheless is stamped with the same "pattern" in that he is fast bound by the traditions of his class and upbringing and is incapable of viewing women as thinking individuals. He knows them only as physical objects and again Meredith states emphatically that this was only "like many of his class and kind." Aminta, then, though so much younger, has left him behind in development and, unlike Diana, she clarifies her values and aims. She realises that independence must be earned. One day as she travels through the suburbs in her carriage "she interestedly observes the cottages and merry gutter children along the squat straight streets . . . Her dominant ultimate thought was 'I too can work'." So when the time comes to make a clean break with her former life and start anew she does not hesitate to shed the ideas of station which she has outgrown: "I had an idea it was glorious. I despise it or rather the woman who had the desire for it."

> " 'But the step down is into the working world.'
> " 'I have the means to live humbly. I want no more except to be taught to work.'
> " 'You have faith in the power of resistance of the woman living alone?'
> " 'It means breathing to me.' "

Not that she was allowed by Meredith to live alone. That was more than the romantic novel readers of the time could be asked to take especially as there was at hand an attractive young lover, Matey Weyburn, who had grown up with Aminta, and really grown up too, not merely pretended to do so by putting on a uniform and starting a bank account like Lord Ormont. The point, however, had been made that Aminta had freed herself of hero worship and dependence and was therefore ready for a true partnership. And so she and her lover go away and live together without marriage apparently happy ever after. True they exiled themselves to Switzerland but they did not mind that, as they wanted to start an international co-educational school, modelled on Meredith's own.

"But the school?" asks Aminta after she has agreed to abscond with Weyburn. "I shall not consider that we are malefactors", replies Matey firmly. "We believe that we are not offending Divine Law." And the skies did not fall but smiled on them. We have travelled far indeed from those poor outcasts, Lady Dedlock and Lady Barnes Newcome and Edith Dombey, who if they could have looked into the fictitional future might have ceased from wringing their despairing hands and instead lifted them up to Heaven in amazement at the sight of merry Matey and Aminta running their respected and flourishing educational establishment.

The book, however, was not a success, was not, in fact, taken very seriously and there is no doubt that Meredith's ideas were ahead of the generally accepted view, but they were none the less representative of the wind of change. With the exception of Rhoda Fleming, Meredith's heroines are all of high degree, but what he did for the great ladies of society, Hardy at the end of the century did for the peasant girl and wife. He and Meredith make a bridge between the Victorian novel proper and the new revolutionary world of H. G. Wells's *Ann Veronica* and Shaw's *Man and Superman*.

8
Across the Atlantic

The Scene in New England

The pioneering nature of life in the early days of American history had, from the first, raised the status of wives from that of subservience to that of partnership. As the settlers pushed further west, the need for resolute and able women spread, and later on the anti-slave movement and the Civil War gave opportunities for initiative and organisation. A better education was provided for girls and they were regarded as culturally equal or even superior to their brothers. New England was the intellectual centre from which civilisation penetrated to the West, and the most influential writers and reformers of the nineteenth century shared a New England upbringing and background.

In 1889 Lucy Larcom, born in 1824 in the State of Maine, published a little book under the title of *A New England Girlhood* which illustrates the striking differences between the influences which surrounded a middle-class girl brought up in that part of America in the first half of the century and her contemporary in England. Lucy Larcom was lucky in her period. The extreme of Calvinistic Puritanism had spent itself. What was healthy in its disciplines remained, but a certain warmth and freedom had crept in, which had not yet deteriorated into luxury or licence. The Larcoms were a humble family, the father keeping a store in the little Massachusetts coast town from which he made a steady income; both poverty and riches alike were unknown in the community. Lucy describes how puzzled she was by some of the terms she came across in the hymns learned by heart to pass away the time during the long sermons she was required to sit through at meetings on Sundays:

> Where e'er I take my walk abroad
> How many poor I see!

> "Now a ragged half-clothed child, or one that could really be called poor was the rarest of all sights—and a beggar! oh, if a real beggar would come along! and what sort of a creature could a 'pampered menial' be? I settled down to the conclusion that rich and poor were book words only."

As a reward for voluntarily learning more than a hundred hymns before she was five, Lucy earned a prize—that of being taught to write by her sister. This pleased her very much, and so, incidentally, had the hymns, for she had allowed her imagination to build freely upon them whenever the meaning was obscure to her tender years:

> I'll go to Jesus though my sin
> Hath like a mountain rose,
> I know his courts, I'll enter in
> Whatever may oppose

conjured up a charming scene—a rose of magical beauty, which she would pick and carry up the mountain to the temple on the summit where King Jesus was enthroned, and present it to him. Such interesting visions softened the rigours of the religious upbringing common to all New England children and therefore accepted by them as part of the natural order. In Lucy's case it was balanced by "an almost unlimited freedom of out-of-doors life". The English children's stories and rhymes, not to speak of the hymns, which came her way were not only mysterious with their "rich men in their castle, the poor men at their gates" but also in the many rules and restrictions which governed their behaviour: "We did not think those English children had so good a time as we did, they had to be so prim and methodical."

Lucy belonged to a large family but her father "had always strongly emphasised his wish that all his children, girls as well as boys, should have some independent means of self-support by the labor of their hands." Each child was encouraged to feel itself a useful part of the family with small tasks to perform for the well-being of all. This was to stand them in good stead, for Lucy's kind and sensible father died comparatively early and the children had to help their mother and each other in earnest. She decided to be a teacher and was sensible of her good fortune in being able to choose what she wanted to do: "When I was young, girls as well as boys had already begun to be encouraged to cultivate and make use of their individual powers."

But her education was by no means a one-sided academic affair. She and her sister, unlike even the poorer middle-class families in England, were used to having no domestic help. As a result, "we learned how to do everything that a woman might be called upon to do under any circumstances for herself or for the household she lived in. It was one of the advantages of the old simple way of living that the young daughters of the home were, as a matter of course, instructed in all these things. They acquired the habit of being ready for emergencies and were delightfully independent."

At about the mid-century a model textile factory for women workers was started in New England called after the poet Lowell. It must have been an extraordinary place. Many of the girls were earning money in order to pay for their education and these attended school or college half the year and the factory the other half, and while their hands were busy their minds were also active in all possible ways. They ran a highbrow magazine—they propped up books of philosophy or poetry on their looms, they attended discussion groups. Lucy joined them for a time and has an illuminating comment to make on the value for a woman, however contented, in getting away from home:

> "Home life is necessarily narrowing. That is one reason why so many women are petty and unthoughtful of any except their own family interests. We have hardly begun to live until we can take in the idea of the whole human family as the one to which we truly belong. To me it was an incalculable help to find myself among so many working girls, all of us thrown upon our own resources."

She adds that in America "no odium could be attached to any honest toil that any self-respecting woman might undertake." She obviously was subject to none. Mary Lyon, the founder of Mount Holyoke Seminary for Women, received several of these "Lowell" girls as students, among whom was Lucy, and very good use they made of their time there. Many of the girls thus trained in New England emigrated to the untamed West as teachers and missionaries, and this is what Lucy herself did.

What a breath of life such an upbringing and education would have been to the mid-Victorian English girl, from the struggling rebellious Florence Nightingales and Maggie Tullivers and Dorothea Brookes with their stifled ambitions to the poor doll-wives debased by false conventions of ignorant gentility and helplessness. To set against Trollope's image of the clinging ivy and the supporting tower as the proper relationship between the sexes, we have New England Lucy Larcom's declaration that "a girl's place in the world is a very strong one and it is a pity she does not always see it so. Her weakness comes from her inclination to lean against something. She often lets her life get broken in fragments when it might be a perfect thing in the upright beauty of its own consecrated freedom." In place of dependence she believed that courage and self-reliance should be the aim of women and her own experience had developed in her just these qualities, but such experience was not possible yet in Europe.

She was particularly lucky in her parents and friends but a similar tone and ideas are to be found in many a New England record, both in fact and in fiction. The women all breathe the same air of independence and idealism. To use Lucy's own term, they are aware of a "consecrated freedom". They make mistakes, of course, but these are their own mistakes for which they feel responsible. They suffer, but they are not helpless; in a word they are active, not passive, and there is a notable lack of the hero-worshipping element among them.

They do not change much during our period. As the years pass they may learn fewer hymns and buy more bonnets, but they remain the same in essence, and Kipling might have been describing the young Harriet Beecher or one of the Alcotts or one of Howells's or Henry James's characters when he wrote in *American Notes* at the end of the century:

> Man is fire and woman is tow
> And the devil he comes and begins to blow.

"In America the tow is soaked in a solution that makes it fireproof—in absolute liberty and large knowledge. But the freedom of the young girl has its drawbacks. She is, I say it with all reluctance—irreverent."

In fact, to the European male the state of affairs seems to be unaccountably topsy-turvy. The hero-worship is accorded the female of the species from youth upwards. Oliver Wendell Holmes in *Elsie Venner* (1861) writes: "The education to all that is beautiful is flowing in mainly through women . . . our young men come into active life so early that if our girls were not educated to something beyond more practical duties, our material prosperity would outstrip our culture." So the hero of his story goes from choice to teach at a girls' school.

163

Nathaniel Hawthorne's sympathy with women is very marked and his best remembered work, that strange story of *The Scarlet Letter* (1850), was written as a parable to show up the greater guilt and weakness of man in a case of adultery. Although the tale is set in an earlier age in order to make the punishment plausible, the moral remains pertinent. The scarlet letter "A" is worn outwardly as a badge of shame by the woman, Hester, but is transmuted, by her loving service for others, into a symbol of charity. The man, whose sin is unacknowledged, carries this letter burnt into his flesh secretly as a sort of evil stigma which in the end destroys him. The people brought all their sorrows to Hester, "as to one who had herself gone through a mightly trouble. Women, more especially— in the continually recurring trials of wounded, wasted, wronged, misplaced or erring and sinful passion—or with the dreary burden of a heart unyielded, because unvalued and unsought—came to her cottage demanding why they were so wretched and what the remedy . . . She assured them of her firm belief that at some brighter period, when the world should have grown ripe for it, a new truth would be revealed, in order to establish the whole relation between man and woman on a surer ground of mutual happiness."

In *The House of the Seven Gables* there is a delightful touch very reminiscent of Lucy Larcom. Phoebe, the heroine, is incarcerated in the old house with her unattractive relatives and, says Hawthorne, "unless she had occasionally obeyed the impulse of nature in New England girls, by attending a metaphysical or philosophical lecture, poor Phoebe would have grown thin."

In his *Blithedale Romance*, another highly symbolic tale based on his actual experiences at the experimental Brook Farm, Hawthorne takes two sisters to represent the two irreconcilable sides of women's character. Zenobia, said to be based on the writer and lecturer Margaret Fuller, is "a portrait of a high-spirited woman, bruising herself against the narrow limitations of her sex." Priscilla is the gentle, pliant, adoring type. It is

Zenobia who comes to a tragic end, but Priscilla's fate, as wife to the egotist Hollingworth, is not much happier.

Hawthorne is obviously fascinated by the problem of women's place in society. There is a discussion on the subject of Blithedale, no doubt reminiscent of the sort of arguments which went on at Brook Farm. "I would give woman all she asks and a great deal more," says one speaker, "which men, if they were generous and wise would grant of their own free motion. For instance, I should love dearly to have all government devolve into the hands of women. It is the iron sway of bodily force which abases us."

With such champions among the men, the American women novelists are clearly much less on the defensive. They are neither as resigned as George Eliot or Mrs Gaskell, nor as dutiful as Miss Yonge. Indeed, the novelists of either sex seem most concerned with their women characters. Occasionally, as in Mrs Harrison's novels, the whole idea of dependence is openly attacked, but for the most part, as in Louisa Alcott's *Good Wives* and in Harriet Beecher Stowe's *Old Town Folk*, marriage is shown to be an equal partnership.

Sarah Orne Jewett, a New England doctor's daughter who used to drive about with her father on his professional visits, stresses, in her simple vivid stories, this quality of mutual help among the humble men and women she grew to know so well.

"These people," she said, "mate, live together and die together in a friendship and felt kinship which is deeper than love. Their marriages are accommodations in response to the needs they recognise they can feel for one another."

Towards the end of the period two of America's foremost novel writers, William Dean Howells and Henry James, are entranced by the subject of the young American girl as contrasted with the product of England, France or Italy. They seem never tired of studying them either in their own home surroundings or in London, Paris or Rome, and it is always their independence and idealism, their innocence, seriousness and determination which are stressed. Sometimes, as in *Daisy Miller* (1878), a situation arises when these qualities, confronted with the far from innocent or idealistic world around, result in a tragic encounter which could never have occurred with the sheltered European girl, but for the most part the young American is quite equal to all emergencies. W. D. Howells's formidable Florida Vervain, in *A Foregone Conclusion* (1875), is a person "wholly abandoned to the truth" without resulting disaster to herself. We immediately think of Clara Middleton's passionate complaint (in Meredith's *The Egoist*) that no women are able to be straightforwardly sincere, however much they may desire it. It is with reference to Florida that Howells, like Hawthorne and Holmes before him, reverses the hero-worship between the sexes, declaring: "It is from women that men take fire and accomplish sublime impossibilities. We need the impulse of pure ideal which we can only get from them." In fact: "She for God only—he for God in her." The "free minds, unashamed and unafraid" of women, are continually extolled by Howells.

James's young heroines are very similar. Bessie Alden is quite able to cope with the English nobility and retain her dignity. She is studied in relation to the European environment. But in the Europeans we are shown how Gertrude and Charlotte Wentworth and Lizzie Acton in their New England home strike the young cosmopolitan Felix. Their simplicity, freedom and seriousness charms him:

> "He had never before found himself in contact so unrestricted with young unmarried ladies. He was extremely fond of the society of ladies and it was new to him that it might be enjoyed in just that manner. His pleasure came from something they had in common. He had known, fortunately, many virtuous gentlewomen, but it now appeared to him that in his relations with them (especially when they were unmarried) he had been looking at pictures under glass. He perceived at present what a nuisance

the glass had been—how it perverted and interfered. He liked so much knowing that he was perfectly at liberty to be alone for hours, anywhere with either of them."

The ease and spontaneity of Milly in *The Wings of a Dove* is emphasised in contrast with English Kate Croy, also her "strong and special implication of liberty of action".

The older married women of Howells and James are also quite different from their European counterparts. They are strong-minded, wealthy and strikingly free of husbands; these are either deceased (like the female spider the American matron seems to have been of a pretty deadly variety) or, at the best, are too busy accumulating riches to accompany their wives and daughters. Two men in Howells's *Open-eyed Conspiracy* are discussing a chance acquaintance:

> " 'I wonder what the mother was like?'
> " 'Yes, evidently she didn't get that will from her father.'
> " 'What do you think it portends for poor Kendricks?'
> " 'What indeed!' "

James's Mrs Touchett, in *Portrait of a Lady* (1881), resembled "a queen-regent or the matron of a gaol". His Mrs Westgate strikes the Englishman as "awfully argumentative. American Ladies certainly don't mind contradicting you. I don't think I was ever treated so by a woman before. She is so devilish positive." Mrs Stringham in *The Wings of a Dove* is neither wealthy or domineering but she *is* an independent cultured Bostonian widow, earning her living as a journalist. There are a few foolish characters among them and when met with their silliness is not considered praiseworthy. Howells has one attractive foolish woman, Mrs Vervain in *A Foregone Conclusion*, but she has character. She could be contrasted with Mrs Nickleby to illustrate the difference in attitude between their creators. Both are talkative, inconsequential creatures with only daughters whom it is their business in life to marry off, but Mrs Vervain is drawn with sympathy: "I don't really seem to have the strength to be sensible. I know it's silly as well as you. The Talk just seems to keep going on of itself—slipping out, slipping out." Her silliness is not genetic but individual and it might just as well have belonged to a man. Moreover she is shown to have pockets of common sense. She is quite a good business woman and is redeemed by being "very much a Bohemian at heart, the gentlest and most blameless of the tribe, but still lawless." No English widow in the same position could afford to be lawless.

The absorbing study of the women of the New World contrated with the old is the subject of one of James's most successful books, his *Portrait of a Lady*. When he wrote it he had lately read and admired George Eliot's novel *Daniel Deronda*, and his Isobel Archer has many points in common with her Gwendolyn Harleth. To conclude this glance at the women of some New England fiction as compared with the corresponding heroines of the English nineteenth-century novel, it may be worthwhile to examine the characters and destinies of Gwendolyn and Isobel in some detail.

Both girls are beautiful, fastidious, intelligent, spoiled by their families and conscious of their superiority to most other women. Both have ambition yet both make disastrous marriages with heartless and selfish men. Each learns—one before, the other after marriage—of her husband's unpleasant pre-marital entanglements. Both too have a strange undefined relationship with another man, Deronda and Ralph Touchett respectively, who acts as a sort of arbiter or fate in their lives. But in spite of these similarities the two are immensely different and this difference arises in part from their different nationality.

Gwendolyn Harleth is the cherished eldest daughter of a meek little widow whose own experience of matrimony has been thoroughly unhappy. The half-consciousness of this has given Gwendolyn herself a supressed fear of marriage, especially of the physical closeness involved which she senses rather than understands, being of course entirely ignorant and inexperienced: "Gwendolyn had about as accurate a conception of marriage . . . as she had of magnetic currents and the law of storms." Especially was she ignorant of the forces within her. When her cousin, Rex, deeply in love with her, tries to take her hand she finds herself quite unexpectedly "passionately averse to this volunteered love". Her mother finds her later sobbing bitterly: "Oh, mamma, what can become of my life? there is nothing worth living for." She was suddenly unbearably oppressed by this claustrophobic pressure to marry which was all the more stifling because there was something dark and mysterious about the whole thing which nobody talked about but which girls felt and feared. Gwendolyn realises, however, that marriage is her inevitable destiny and builds a fantasy of possible luxury and power around the idea. Her duty in exploiting her charm in order to make a good, in other words, a prosperous marriage, is also impressed upon her by her uncle, the rector.

She answers his exhortation thus:

"I know I must be married sometime before it is too late. And I don't see how I could do better than marry Mr Grandcourt. I mean to accept him if possible." (Mr Grandcourt is from worldly prospects an exceedingly eligible young man.) Her uncle is slightly shocked at her matter-of-fact approach to the subject which swept aside the sentimentality with which the Victorian male liked to surround it. "My dear Gwendolyn," he answers, "I trust that you will find in marriage a new form of duty and affection. Marriage is the only true and satisfactory sphere of a woman."

With Isobel Archer, on the other hand, we are in a more spacious world and her relatives take up a precisely opposite attitude. Her aunt, Mrs Touchett, could hardly differ more strikingly from Gwendolyn's poor downtrodden mother. It would indeed be impossible to find her like in any English novel. She is completely independent and "likes to do everything for herself". She lives apart from her husband but she appears to perceive nothing irregular in the situation. She makes him and her son periodic visits. On being asked what she intends to do with her niece she replies: "Do with her? You talk as if she were a yard of calico. I shall do absolutely nothing with her and she herself will do everything she chooses. Marry her? I should be sorry to play her such a trick." We see later on that Mr Touchett too and her cousin Ralph are equally unwilling to marry off Isobel while she herself (though to begin with she is as poor as Gwendolyn) by no means looks upon it as her inescapable lot. "I am very fond of my liberty", she states, not wistfully but explicitly.

At the outset, then, Gwendolyn's choice in life is a narrow one and the influences surrounding her all point in one direction. The American girl believes herself to be a free agent and is treated as one. She has already refused a "good offer" in her own country and now she refuses Lord Warburton, an irreproachable English peer, a far more attractive and desirable husband than Gwendolyn's Grandcourt. She refuses him, moreover, not because she dislikes him nor from any innate disinclination to marriage but for the sake of that same much-prized liberty of hers.

Gwendolyn is attracted to Grandcourt not only because he is the great "catch" of the neighbourhood, to secure whom would be a personal triumph, but also ironically because his cold undemonstrative nature does not arouse her hidden and frightening revulsion to marriage. With a delicious and endearing boasting she declares: "How I pity all the other girls at the Archery Meeting—all thinking of Mr Grandcourt! and they have not a shadow of a chance, now you know they have not, mamma." In the light of what we know of Grandcourt, we can hardly bear this pretty flaunting.

On the eve of becoming engaged, however, Gwendolyn learns that Grandcourt has had a liaison for many years with a beautiful and cultured woman who has loved him faithfully and borne him four children. She is horrified, promises this woman never to marry him and breaks off contact with him. Now fate intervenes, her family suffers a severe financial loss and Grandcourt, undeterred by this, renews the chase to the admiration of all Gwendolyn's relations and friends. Nothing is in store for her, should she not accept him, but a life of uncongenial toil as a governess. It is not only uncongenial but she has been taught to look upon it as degrading. Isobel Archer would not have done so. In Louisa Alcott's *Little Women*, American Meg goes for a picnic with some visiting English young ladies and, admiring the sketching of one of these, is asked: "Why don't you learn?"

> " 'I haven't time.'
> " 'Can't you persuade your governess?'
> " 'I have none.'
> " 'I forgot; young ladies in America go to school more than with us.'
> " 'I don't go at all, I am a governess myself.'
> " 'Oh, indeed!' said Miss Kate; but she might as well have said, 'Dear me, how dreadful'—for her tone implied it, and something in her face made Meg colour, and wish she had not been so frank.
> "Mr Brooke looked up, and said quietly, 'Young ladies in America love independence as much as their ancestors did, and are admired and respected for supporting themselves.'
> " 'Oh, yes; of course it's very nice and proper in them to do so. We have many most respectable and worthy young women who do the same . . .' said Miss Kate, in a patronizing tone . . . that made Meg's work seem not only more distasteful, but degrading."

To Gwendolyn, to become one of these respectable and worthy young women seemed unbearable. Life in a small cottage with her mother and sisters seemed equally unbearable. Her character, her upbringing, her vanity, even the affection she bore her mother all urged her to capitulate. The scales are weighted against her but still there is a moral choice to be made and she allows herself to evade her conscience and to slide into the wrong course. George Eliot sees to it that the issues are plainly though compassionately stated.

Now we do not know anything like so much about Isobel Archer as about Gwendolyn because we only see her as did her creator, from without, but we do know enough to be certain that faced with the same knowledge and the same set of circumstances, nothing would have induced Isobel to marry Grandcourt. She is, for one thing, thoroughly endued with American idealism. Stemming from the New England tradition this idealism, now perhaps lacking its initial disciplines, has its own dangers. It would have prevented her, if nothing else did, from Gwendolyn's pitiful compromising with her conscience but it also actually led to her own downfall. Yet Isobel's mistake could hardly be said to be a moral one. The only reproach that can be levelled at her is that of trusting too much to her own judgement. This self-confidence, like her idealism, is part of her heritage. Early in her visit to England she is told by her aunt: "Young girls here don't sit alone with the gentlemen late at night."

"You were very right to tell me then," she said. "I don't understand it but I am very glad to know it. I always want to know the things one shouldn't do."

"So as to do them?"

"So as to choose."

This self-confidence, together with her charm, so infects Ralph Touchett that he persuades his father to leave her a fortune that she may be free indeed to choose her own destiny. She chooses to marry Mr Osmond, an effete egotist, an expatriate living in Italy, whom she clothes with a sort of potential nobility, that she believes she may help him to realise.

It is a measure of James's partial failure that, although we believe in Isobel's sincerity, we cannot quite credit her with the stupidity involved in this appalling blunder. She is not in love with Osmond any more than with Lord Warburton. Whereas Gwendolyn's tragedy is only too convincing, Isobel's, in choosing marriage with Osmond as her experiment in idealism, leaves us puzzled. It mystifies her friends no less than us. Henrietta Stackpole, the professional woman journalist (another character impossible to meet in the contemporary English novel), considered that "there is something very low in the tone of Europeans towards women" and distrusted and disliked Osmond from the first, and Ralph Touchett is deeply disappointed and troubled. "A year ago", he says, "you valued your liberty beyond everything." "What had become of all her ardour, her aspirations, her theories, her high estimate of her independence and her incipient conviction that she should never marry?"

What indeed? Whereas the whole tone of Gwendolyn's character, upbringing and the attitude of her family and acquaintances make her choice all but inevitable, the same elements make Isobel's seem arbitrary. Their subsequent behaviour however is consistent. The very fact that Isobel had been able to form all these theories of independence made her also able to retain sufficient freedom of thought and behaviour after marriage to keep her self-respect. Also she had nothing but stupidity to reproach herself with and, most important, she kept control of her fortune, a legal impossibility for Gwendolyn as an Englishwoman, even had she possessed one.*

Hatred and despair quickly engulf poor Gwendolyn after marriage and, unable to stand alone, she turns for support to Daniel Deronda, who becomes for her a sort of saviour. Isobel, who disdains Ralph's advice before marriage, does not seek it afterwards, though the consciousness of what he means to her grows.

Gwendolyn could never have escaped from Grandcourt but by his death, and she longs for this and fears her own longing. At last a terrible second choice is given her. He is in danger of drowning and her hesitation in throwing him a rope, though momentary, is fatal. She pours out her remorse and her guilt

* Married Woman's Property Act in New England—1847; in England—1882.

to Deronda: "You must not forsake me. I will bear any penance . . . but you must not forsake me." She is relegated by Deronda to the only life that George Eliot now sees possible for her, a quiet redemption by self-sacrifice for others.

Isobel's release comes from a deliberate defying of her husband's orders. She wishes to go to England to Ralph who is dying. Osmond has forbidden her to go. "Ah," cried her sister-in-law enviously, "when I want to make a journey my husband simply tells me I can have no money." Her second choice now comes to Isobel. What decides her to defy her husband is the opportune revelation of the use that he and his former mistress, Madame Merle, have made of her in furthering their own plans. She is altogether luckier than Gwendolyn. She makes the right choice and henceforth at least is free in spirit. Gwendolyn is forced to yield Deronda up to another woman, Isobel only yields Ralph up to death. When he is dying he confesses that it was by his doing that she inherited the fortune that led to her marriage. "I believe I ruined you", he says. But she was not ruined. Gwendolyn was the slave woman driven to desperate hatred. Isobel never became a slave and even among the ruins of her marriage some self-confidence remains: "To live only to suffer—it seemed to her she was too valuable, too capable for that." It seemed so to Ralph also: "I don't believe that such a generous mistake as yours can hurt you for more than a little."

Like several of Henry James's stories, *The Portrait of a Lady* ends in ambiguity. Isobel returns to Osmond after Ralph's death but it is Henrietta Stackpole who has the last word. She, who had always urged Isobel to leave her husband—"nothing is more common in our Western cities, and it is to them after all that we must look in the future"—she it is who addresses to Casper Goodwood, Isobel's first and most faithful suitor, the final sentence of the book: "Look here, Mr Goodwood, you just wait."

Gwendolyn Harleth and Isobel Archer are distinct and differing personalities and their reactions to their destiny as women were determined largely by their characters, but how far these were influenced by their differing national environment it is not possible to measure. That Henry James wished to make certain aspects of these differences explicit is clear. Indeed, he sometimes gives an almost allegorical significance to the comparison. Casper Goodwood stands for the New World, full of crude energy and determination, and Osmond for the still beautiful but decadent Europe to whom Isobel is determined to bring new life and power. Henrietta Stackpole and Pansy Osmond, Isobel's stepdaughter, can also be taken as symbolic figures, the one of the new brash independent woman, the other as the epitome of the gentle, obedient, helpless innocence which was the European ideal of girlhood. This allegorical approach begs the question of Isobel's dilemma. The truth is that James has made all his characters too real for any such symbolism to carry conviction. But its shadowy presence emphasises the contrast between the two worlds.

Harriet Beecher Stowe
1811-1896

Harriet Beecher Stowe was the author of the most socially influential novel ever written. She herself claimed that *Uncle
Tom's Cabin* was dictated to her by God Himself. "How odd of
God to choose a woman for such a task" was probably the
thought in the minds of many a Victorian Englishman, but this
would not have occurred to Mrs Stowe's own countrymen and
certainly not to herself. One of the characters in her last book—
Old Town Folks—Minerva Randall, was of the opinion that "if
women want any rights they had better take them and say
nothing about it. Her sex had never occurred to her as a reason
for doing or not doing anything which her hand found to do."
The same might be said of her creator.

It was not with her sex but a far more serious discrimination with which she found herself involved from childhood
upwards. Was she destined for heaven or for hell?—could she
count herself as one of the elect? Her father, Lyman Beecher, a
Calvinist minister, made no distinction between his sons and
his daughters. Each was an immortal soul with an eternal destiny of which he was passionately and perpetually aware. They
were certainly a family worth troubling about, from Catherine
the eldest, who wrote philosophic pamphlets that confounded
German professors, to Isabella the youngest, who became an
advanced feminist defending "free love" as "a noble personal

independence", with Henry Ward Beecher, whom Lincoln once declared to be the greatest of his countrymen, and Harriet, the world-renowned author of *Uncle Tom's Cabin*, thrown in as good measure.

Lyman Beecher himself was a splendid preacher and a man of vivid personality and his first wife was his equal in all-round ability. She had learned mathematics, physics and chemistry—"I suppose you know of the discovery that the fixed alcalies are metallic oxyd", she wrote casually to her sister. She was also a good artist and craftswoman. She had eight children, spun, wove and cooked for them and kept a school. She was a woman who believed in rigid discipline, independence and integrity. She died of consumption, swiftly, serenely, and self-confidently, and forty years after her death her husband could not hear her name spoken without strong emotion—though he married again, also a woman of strong character and good sense.

Such parents could not fail to leave their mark on their children. Lyman himself, though so intense and fiery that a small boy once said to him, "Sir, I think you must be Appollyon", was devoted to them all and this forged yet another link in the fetters with which his faith sought to bind them. They had to break free. Henry was probably irreparably injured by the conflict, for all his brilliant gifts could not save him from an underlying indecision and vagueness which were the result of his father's early domination. Catherine achieved independence through her sound and capable intellect. Harriet, a simpler character, while still very young underwent a joyful spiritual experience which she felt was a sign that all was well, but doubts crept in; her sister's influence told and there was much despondency and conflict before she evolved a philosophy compounded of imagination and emotion to displace the harsh Calvinist doctrine which continued, however, to haunt her throughout life.

The struggle to come to terms with the terrible logic of these New England preachers is the theme of two of her latest books —*The Minister's Wooing* and *Old Town Folks*. In them she quotes from actual passages of sermons heard or read by the young Beechers: "All the use which God will have for the greater part of mankind is to suffer: therefore all their faculties and their whole capacities will be employed and used for this end . . . The body can by omnipotence be made capable of suffering the greatest imaginable pain for eternity without producing dissolution." The men who preached such shocking stuff were by no means heartless themselves. They were not made in the image of their god. One of them set apart days of fasting "in which he was wont to walk the floor weeping and wringing his hands at the thought of 'the dreadful doom of the lost'." But their obvious sincerity must have only made matters worse. Lyman Beecher was certainly deeply affected by the doctrinal teaching of his day but he was also a naturally benevolent and hopeful man, who, though longing for assurance, yet allowed himself to hope that his children were among the elect. He was also responsible for passing on to all of them a capacity for leadership, a belief in themselves, a fervour in action and the inability to accept defeat.

Unlike the Maggie Tullivers and the Florence Nightingales of the Old World, Harriet was never denied the education her lively mind demanded. A description of the school at Cloudland in *Old Town Folks* is founded on the Female Academy at Litchfield where Harriet went as a child. It was for both boys and girls, the pupils jointly studying Latin, history, geography and mathematics. Needless to say, theology was also taught and Harriet, when twelve years old, wrote an essay debating "Can the Immortality of the Soul be proved by the Light of Nature?" The boys and girls also acted plays together which, even though the subjects were always Biblical, provided plenty of opportunity for shared fun, ingenuity and responsibility. From this school Harriet went to help Catherine as a pupil teacher in the school she had started which had good academic standards.

When Harriet was twenty-one, her father felt a call to become principal of a newly established seminary at Cincinnati (not long before the Trollopes started their ill-fated venture in the same town). One friend came with them to help Lyman; this was Professor Stowe, a scholar in Hebrew, lately married to a clever young wife who died of cholera soon after their arrival. Professor Stowe, never a sanguine man, was wretched, mourning his wife, hating Cincinnati, depressed by the uncertain prospects of the seminary. The determination of Lyman Beecher held him there against his will; and the no less firm purpose of Harriet Beecher to rescue him from his misery resulted in their marriage.

Harriet was not, as far as one can gather, at all in love. She did not need a home, she hated domesticity, she was far too independent ever to require a man as a prop. Why then did she marry Stowe? She afterwards said it was the influence of her adored brother Henry (who was very fond of the Professor) "which ended in making me a wife". Henry probably put the idea into her head, but she was a Beecher, she loved adventure, change, excitement; she also loved to shape her own destiny and those of others, to exercise power, not without a certain humility, but with confidence. There might too have been the attraction of opposites. He was old for his age, large, unwieldy, given to melancholy, somewhat indecisive and helpless. She was young, small and lively, decided and self-confident. Their marriage might have been a failure but it was not subject to quite the same strains and limitations that an exceptionally endowed woman married to a retiring and valetudinous scholar would have met with in Europe.

There were, of course, the inescapable strains of motherhood and, for a time, of comparative poverty. Babies came with a rush, Professor Stowe's salary was precarious and her work of looking after the children, making and mending, seemed unending. She did not suffer in silence and never accepted the unpleasantness of life patiently. "Indeed, my dear, I am but a mere drudge", she wrote to a friend, and again: "I am sick of the smell of sour milk and sour meat and sour everything." All the same, she found time to write endless letters and even some short stories and sketches. There is a sketch called "A Scholar's Adventure in the Country" where the husband's impractical nature is shown up in contrast to his wife's resources and responsibility: it was published without Professor Stowe's knowledge.

"I am not calculated to endure great pressure of care," she wrote to him. "I am probably not destined for a long life." But when he in his turn tried the effect of a little self-pity he received short shrift from her. "My dear soul," she wrote, "I received your most melancholy effusion, and I am sorry to find it so. Why didn't you engage two tombstones—one for you and one for me? But, seriously, my dear husband, you must try and be patient . . . To see things as through a glass darkly is your infirmity, you know."

This curiously comic pattern is often repeated in letters between them, for neither of them had any hesitation in leaving the other, if the spirit so moved them, and, for an affectionate couple, the time they spent apart cannot but strike the reader with wonder. First Professor Stowe goes east, ostensibly to try and whip up funds for the seminary, but he is obviously enjoying the holiday from Cincinnati to the full. Then Harriet goes off for eleven months to try a water cure. When she comes back he, not to be outdone, goes off in his turn for the same treatment for fifteen months. While he is away the children are all ill and the baby Charley dies of cholera but "as regards your coming home", writes Harriet firmly, "I am decidedly opposed to it."

At last an opportunity arose for Professor Stowe to leave the seminary and to move to Bowdon College, Brunswick, but he had to wait until his place at the school could be filled, so off went Harriet again, impatient for the change, to settle herself with three out of the five children in a new home. She lets everyone, including her husband, know how much she has to do, how well she does it, how feeble is her health, how indispensable her presence, how strong her will, and through it all shines her enjoyment of activity, power and variety. "To come alone", she writes—but she was not alone in our sense of the word, she had a "faithful female friend" who helped her through all emergencies, and she also had plenty of domestic help—"To come alone such a distance with the whole charge of children, accounts and baggage has been a very severe trial of my strength," etc., etc., but also, "My dear husband, trust all to me; I never doubt or despair." A little later a terrific letter to her sister-in-law describes her settling in "and then comes a letter from my husband saying he is sick abed and all but dead; don't ever expect to see his family again; wants to know how I shall manage in case I am left a widow; knows we shall get into debt, warns me to be prudent. I read the letter and poke it into the fire."

The Beecher spirit prevailed, she painted, prepared, laid carpets, made chairs, and the household was collected together. Finally Professor Stowe arrived and the last and sixth child was born. But soon after another sort of child came into being, the child of her brain, whether dictated by God or not, certainly miraculously scribbled on the kitchen table in the midst of the family with neither comfort nor privacy—*Uncle Tom's Cabin*, a shattering creation which, sweeping across two continents, left a trail of passionate emotion in its wake.

The response to the anti-slavery agitation on the part of the Beecher family was curiously ambivalent. Lyman Beecher seems to have largely ignored it. His influence might have carried the day among the churches, but he was convinced that the end of the world was not far off, so that to spend himself in such a cause was superfluous. Henry Ward Beecher, his famous son, at first attached himself to the liberal anti-slavery party chiefly because of its opposition to the strict Calvinists, and finally plunged into the abolitionist movement with all the strength of his emotional and dramatic personality. He improvised a slave auction as a sort of stage show and roused his audience to a frenzy, but he never became an out and out abolitionist, and after the Civil War was over, incurred great unpopularity by sympathising with the South.

As to Harriet herself, she too, at first, was not apparently particularly interested in the slave question, certainly not so concerned as she was with the controversy over Calvinistic theology. It was the operation of the Fugitive Slave Law with which she had happened to come into personal contact which aroused her passionate sympathy, but she seemed to write under a strong emotional compulsion which had little to do with any reasoned "cause" and not to realise at all that her book was a powerful abolitionist manifesto.

To decry *Uncle Tom's Cabin* as a sentimental piece of propaganda would be an utterly wrong judgement. There is a width of canvas, including the vivid description of certain scenes, that one would hardly expect from a "woman writer"—a Kentucky village bar, for instance, where all the talk between the slave trader, Haley, and his associates rings convincingly true. The characters of the Calvinist Aunt Ophelia, of the irrepressible Topsy and of the elegant, unhappy St Clare, are all naturally drawn. But Harriet was not her father's child for nothing and the symbolic figures of pure good and pure evil in the persons of little Eva and Uncle Tom on the one side, and the brutal Legree on the other, dominate the story. The death-beds of angels and devils were much to the taste of nineteenth-century readers, and they found Uncle Tom's death particularly irresistible.

Harriet's accounts of the composition of this scene are variable but always told with strong emotion. At one time she describes how "the scene presented itself almost as a tangible vision to my mind while sitting at the Communion Table in Brunswick Church." She was shaken by sobs and hurried home; her husband being absent, she read it to her two little boys, who, not without much gratification to their mother, "broke out into convulsions of weeping". In another account she tells how the vision came upon her while her husband slept: "Just as I had finished writing it down Mr Stowe awoke. 'Wife,' said he, 'have you not lain down yet?' 'No,' I answered, 'I have been writing and I want you to listen to this and see if it will do.' I read aloud to him with the tears flowing fast. He wept too and before I had finished his sobs shook the bed upon which he was lying." Whichever is the correct tale hardly matters. The vision was the same and the weeping. What *has* happened to our tear ducts in the last hundred years?

From the very first there was no doubt whatever of the book's impact. Ten thousand copies were sold within a few days of its publication in 1852, and over three hundred thousand within a year. "Pure, penetrating and profound", declared George Sand, voicing the opinion of Europe; "noble, generous and great the heart which embraces in her pity, in her love, an entire race, trodden down in blood and mire under the whip of ruffians and the maledictions of the impious." Harriet herself should hardly have been surprised at the reception of the book considering her firm conviction that she was directly inspired:

> "I did not write it."
> "What! you did not write Uncle Tom?"
> "No, I only put down what I saw."
> "But, you have never been in the South!"
> "No, but it all came before me and I put it down in words."

She was surprised, however, at the reaction of the Abolitionists, whom she had expected would not consider it extreme enough, but who on the contrary saw it as the most wonderful piece of propaganda that would ever come their way, and she was equally taken aback by the attitude of the Southerners, whom she had supposed would be pleased by the favourable light in which some of the slave owners had been pictured, but who were universally outraged by the book.

Fame brought freedom from financial stress to the Stowes, and there was no meek handing over of cheques from wife to husband as in the case of the Rev and Mrs Gaskell. There is every evidence that Harriet did what she liked with her money and that she much enjoyed spending it. For the rest her success intensified without changing what had always been present. She had always wished to write, now her career as an author was assured. She had always wanted to help those in trouble, now she had the immense satisfaction of opportunity and fulfilment. She had always been forceful and energetic, now she became more so. She was accustomed to long periods of separation from her husband, now these became even more frequent and justifiable. If she gloried in her notoriety, it did not noticeably change her or embitter him. "Dear One," she writes while abroad on a long public visit, "if this effort impedes my journey home and wastes some of my strength, you will not murmur, I feel a sacred call to be the helper of the helpless." He did murmur, but she took no notice. She had never taken much notice and he probably did not expect it. She did take him with her to Scotland, however, and there he *was* of use. The prejudice in Europe was so strong against ladies speaking in public meetings that she was forced to employ him to speak for her.

He was not very happy though, trailing in the wake of his wife's almost royal progressions and soon escaped and went home to his studies. He had now become Professor of Sacred Studies at Andover Theological Seminary. He was "my poor old Rabbi" or "Rab" to her then and remained so to the end. She herself went on from strength to strength. Three chief friendships that she formed with notable Englishwomen are perhaps significant: George Eliot, whose relationship with George Lewis put her outside the pale of English polite society; Elizabeth Barrett, whose marriage with Robert Browning was unique in its absolute equality of status between the two; and Lady Byron, who had become in her mind a symbol of enslaved womanhood. After Lady Byron's death, she rushed passionately and somewhat injudiciously into print on her behalf and against "the enslavement of women in England where all literature seems to imply that it is no matter what becomes of the *woman* when the man's story is to be told", and railed against "the utter deadness to the sense of justice which the laws, literature and misunderstood religion of England have sought to induce in women as a special grace and virtue". She incurred a good deal of criticism in England for this outburst, but none of the Beechers could refrain from words, and a good many words at that, where they felt strongly.

Harriet's second novel *Dred*, designed to show the effect of slavery on society, was published in 1856, and from Dunrobin Castle, the seat of the Duke and Duchess of Sutherland where she was staying on her second visit to Europe, she wrote to her husband : " 'Dred' is selling over here wonderfully. I am showered with letters private and printed"; and a little later: "One hundred thousand copies sold in four weeks! After that, who cares what the critics say." They said a number of unpleasant things, amongst them that "the author knows nothing of the Society she describes". But Queen Victoria and Harriet Martineau preferred *Dred* to *Uncle Tom's Cabin* and there is no doubt that it fostered and deepened the antagonism to slavery among its many thousands of readers.

This European visit marks perhaps the summit of Mrs Stowe's happiness and fame. On her return home the great personal tragedy of her life, the drowning of her favourite son Henry, and then the great national tragedy of the Civil War, for which she could not help feeling some responsibility, darkened her life. "So you are the little woman who made this great War", President Lincoln said to her. Between the loss of Henry and the start of the War, she went abroad again for a year, without either husband or children, except for the first month or two. In Florence, under the influence of Mrs Browning, she experimented with spiritualism. Professor Stowe did not have to travel to Italy, nor to employ mediums for his own extra-sensory experience. Again they entered into a curious sort of rivalry. "What you said about feeling the presence of dear Henry with you, and, above all, the vibration of that mysterious guitar, was very pleasant to me", she writes; ". . . I cannot, however, think that Henry strikes the guitar, that must be Eliza. Her spirit has ever seemed to cling to that mode of manifestation, and if you would keep it in your sleeping room no doubt you would hear from it oftener."

Her attitude towards her husband here, as often, seems to be that of impatient and ironic affection. "Mr Stowe preached a sermon", she once wrote, "to show that Christ is going to put everything right at last, which is comforting."

Neither war nor personal loss really changed Harriet. She still wrote letters and articles and talked and travelled indefatigably. She still planned new homes and moved her family into them—a large house went up at Hartford, where she had been at school, and then an estate was bought in Florida where her son Frederick might recover from his part in the fighting and where her old Rab might rest. (But Frederick, who was an alcoholic, disappeared one day and was never heard of again.)

The Florida home was a source of great pleasure and contentment to the Stowes: "We are all well, contented and happy here and we have six birds, two dogs and a pony—rooms fragrant with violets, banked up in hyacinths, flowers everywhere, windows open, birds singing." It might have been expected that among such peace and beauty she would have produced her stories with greater facility than amid comparative poverty and the distractions of a young family, but such was not the case and *Old Town Folks*, the last of her books to achieve fame,* was a long while appearing. She thought of it as her masterpiece, at any rate from the literary angle, and it is far less of a sermon than *Uncle Tom's Cabin* or *Dred*.

Old Town Folks is a mellow book and (though the baleful effect of Calvinism is still haunting Harriet and indeed the strangest and darkest of the New England Calvinist preachers, Nathaniel Emmons, is present in the story as Dr Stern) the triumph of love over logic is the underlying theme. Lyman Stowe as Mr Avery is also one of the characters, but shown in his most attractive light: "I have the image of the dear good man now, as I have seen him, seated on a hay-cart, mending

* Neither *The Minister's Wooing* nor *The Pearl of Orr's Island*, both New England novels, were so successful as *Old Town Folks*.

a hoe-handle, and at the same moment vehemently explaining to an inquiring brother minister the exact way that Satan first came to fall as illustrating how a perfectly holy mind can be tempted to sin. The familiarity that he showed with the celestial arcana—the zeal with which he vindicated his Maker —the perfect knowledge that he seemed to have of the strategic plans of the evil powers . . . seemed as vivid and as much a matter of course to his mind as if he had read them out of a weekly newspaper . . . Mr Avery was a firm believer in hell, but he believed also that nobody need go there, and he was determined, so far as he was concerned, that nobody should go there if he could help it." This lighter touch in dealing with the Calvinist theology softens the tragic undertones. "What's life for? Why, for hard work, I s'pose," says the harsh old Miss Asphyxia. "Talk about coddling! it's little we get o'that, the way the Lord fixes things in this world, dear knows . . . and if Mrs Badger does think I've got a heart of stone, I should like to know how I'm to have any other when I ain't elected, and I don't see as I am, or likely to be."

But if *Old Town Folks* is still read with pleasure by those lucky enough to fall in with it, it is not for the theology, nor for the story, but for the pictures of early nineteenth-century New England life that it gives and for some of the strong humorous Puritan characters, with their racy talk and their country wisdom. The true drama of the book is not in the rather melodramatic plot but in the natural drama of the seasons, the bitter long winters, the longed-for springs and the gorgeous summers and autumns, with their appropriate village activities, the minister's "Woodspell", Easter and Thanksgiving. These scenes and these characters were drawn from Harriet's own memories of her father's stories, and of her maternal grandmother's home, Nutplains, but most of all perhaps from the reminiscences of Professor Stowe, who had a lively recollection of his own New England childhood. Over this book there was a real collaboration between husband and wife for Professor Calvin Stowe was no nonentity. It was not easy to be the husband of a celebrity but he continued to be a personality in his own right. In a letter to George Eliot from Florida, Harriet writes: "My poor rabbi—he sends you some Arabic which I fear you cannot read: on diablerie he is up to his ears in knowledge, having read all things in all tongues, from the Talmud down."

The next collaboration in fact was an article on the Talmud for which she laboriously copied out all his Chaldean characters for him and which she goaded him into publishing. Another long separation, though, was embarked upon by Harriet after the publication of *Old Town Folks*. Extravagance had wasted her means and the remedy was obvious and sure, and as she describes it "as easy a way of making money as I have ever tried"—a lengthy tour of readings from her own books. Travelling, however, was arduous, distances immense, and she was by now past sixty years old, but the response was gratifying. People made long journeys to hear her and she was specially pleased when a little Harriet and a little Eva were brought forward for her blessing and when one old deaf woman said to her, "I come just to see you. I'd rather see you than the Queen." But she was worth hearing. Before one of her early readings she brushed up her hair to make herself look like her father—that father the memory of whom had never left her— "Now I look exactly like him when he was going to preach and I shall not fail." She, like her brother Henry, had undoubtedly inherited dramatic power and she could make her audience laugh and cry. Between the acts she would write to her husband in answer to his often reiterated, characteristic "last words": "Now, my dear husband, please do *want* and try to remain with us yet a while longer and let us have a little quiet evening before either of us crosses the river."

She was beginning to wish for that quiet evening, to relish "the love of the old for each other"—to look forward to "some more of our good long talks." For the truth was they were more companionable when they *were* together than many a solidly stay-at-home couple. In spite of the obvious contrasts in their characters, she always the active and he the passive, they appear sometimes to be the two sides of the same medal and to share many rather odd characteristics. Both are hypochondriac, vying with each other in pouring out their complaints of physical miseries. Both, too, exchange visions, but without much interest in each other's experience. He was indeed accustomed to psychical phenomena since the time when as a child he found a blue skeleton sharing his bed (an experience one would have thought to unhinge him for life, but none of his appearances were fraught with terror and they were accepted by him and his family with a curious matter-of-factness). Her visions, however, except for *Uncle Tom*, were dependent on mediums. Both husband and wife were impractical, for though Harriet prided herself on being the practical one of the family, her standards in this direction were not high to say the least of it and she was always absent-minded. There is an endearing story, for instance, of her arrival for the first time at the house of President Quincey Adams. She was escorted to her room with dignity and the ladies of the household waited for her below. They waited in vain, dinner was announced, still no Mrs Stowe. At last the maid was asked to knock on her door but there was no reply. Then Mrs Adams, thinking something must be seriously wrong, hurried up and into the room: "There she stood, bonnet and shawl still on, standing before a bookcase reading a volume which she had taken down. 'Oh!', said she, returning suddenly to the present, 'do forgive me! I found this dear old copy of "Sir Charles Grandison", just like the one I used to read. I haven't seen it for years and years!'"

After the reading tours were finished, shadows began to gather. She was saddened and infuriated by the scandal that arose around the reputation of her famous brother, Henry Ward Beecher, who was accused of adultery with the wife of a well known New York editor. He was acquitted but his reputation was irrevocably tarnished. Her youngest daughter died. They had to give up the Florida home because Professor Stowe was no longer equal to the journeying it involved. Never one to forego self-pity, she exclaims to a friend: "I have been very unwell the season past. I have suffered more pain, more weariness and weakness than ever in my life before ... But one thing I cannot do, while my husband lives, I cannot visit and leave him, neither can I take him." While like a fainter chorus his voice, querulous to the last, complains that the Lord has forgotten him. Yet these outbursts are not offensive because, on her side at least, they are accompanied by courage and a recognition of comfort as well as of misery. "I think we have never enjoyed each other's society more than this winter"; and again: "My two daughters relieve me of every household care and a trained hospital nurse who knows how to do everything, does it with neatness, order and efficiency."

Her husband died after not more than a year of invalidism. Harriet was to outlive him by another ten years, but it is perhaps significant that the flame of life in her burnt only feebly after his death. What they meant to each other it is not easy for an outsider to guess. There was certainly no great flowering of romance in this marriage, but it was a reality and it endured. It was founded on a free and equal relationship and the fact that she was the dominant partner was not to be twisted by social pressures into appearing otherwise.

Abba Alcott
1800-1877

Mrs Alcott was in reality not much like the portrait her famous daughter drew of her as Mrs March in *Little Women*. Jo March's "Marmee" was a motherly domesticated woman, a sweet-tempered, loving, fulfilled wife. Abba Alcott was restless, hot-tempered, possessive, disliking home duties and often neglectful of them, unsatisfied and critical of her husband. Louisa had to create that ideal picture of married life out of the lack of it in reality.

Abba's marriage had been a late one. She was physically attracted to the handsome philosopher and he by the personality of this strong-minded woman who was better educated and connected than himself. There was however no deep affinity between them though they shared at first a combination of rashness. What Abba really thought her life with Bronson would be like it is hard to say, but she certainly did not expect the failure and hardship that attended it. Two ventures in schoolmastery failed, the first through the praiseworthy originality of Bronson's experiments and his refusal to compromise; the second through the unlooked-for death of a patron. Abba, who never understood or approved of her husband's ideas, became disillusioned and bitter. Four daughters had been born to them and after that she decided there should be no more. Not for her the overflowing nurseries of the Victorian wife. She was not maternal by nature and when the children were tiny their father attended to them more tenderly and carefully than their mother. There is a sort of self-consciousness about Abba's motherhood: the fact that she was in the habit of writing little notes to her daughters rather than speaking directly to them when she had anything important to say intensifies this impression, and she even ended one of these notes to a child of eleven: "I am a busy woman, but never can forget the calls of my children".

As a matter of fact the children were left very much on their own and Louisa, who was adventurous, was lost more than once. On one occasion when only three years old she was rescued from drowning in a pond by a casual passer-by, on another, discovered asleep on a doorstep. Both parents were indiscriminately philanthropic. Bronson led the way in giving, sometimes parting with both food and fuel when his own children were in danger of hunger and cold, but Abba brought smallpox into the house from one poor family and later on scarlet fever from another. This latter infection resulted in a tragedy for which she never forgave herself; her third daughter, the Beth of *Little Women*, contracted the illness so badly that she never regained strength and died two years later. It is significant that Louisa, in the book, entirely removes the responsibility for this from her mother and divides it instead between Jo and Beth herself, the incident happening while "Marmee" was away. This impractical philanthropy and the insecurity it involved often came hard on the children. "More people coming to live with us," wrote the child Louisa, in desperation; "I wish we could be together, and no one else. I don't see who is to clothe and feed us all, when we are so poor now."

The completely unconventional upbringing to which the children were subjected was continued into their adolescence. They were allowed to mix freely with the poor and outcast whom Abba occasionally brought home when she was employed as a social worker. When the neighbours ventured to remonstrate she replied proudly: "I can trust my daughters and this is the best way to teach them how to share these sins and comfort these sorrows." There was much to admire in all this if only it had been balanced by precaution, but there is ample evidence both from Louisa's diaries and from her breakdowns in after life that the children suffered. The worst time of insecurity was during the experiment in community living at Fruitlands, Harvard.

After the unsuccessful periods of schooling, husband and wife had drawn apart and Bronson, perhaps welcoming the chance to escape from the disappointed and unhappy Abba, took a trip to Europe financed by Emerson. There he met and brought back with him an enthusiastic disciple, Charles Lane. With Lane's money a farm was bought at Harvard which they renamed Fruitlands and where they hoped to establish a community on the lines of Brook Farm, though it was to be more extreme in its insistence on the manual labour and the very plain living which was to accompany the very high thinking. The drawbacks were that no one either liked or was proficient in manual labour. The experiment lasted only from June to December and was a complete failure. Not only was all Lane's money wasted but Abba was worn out and exasperated by household cares and there were also quarrels arising from emotional discord between herself and Bronson and Lane.

Nearby Fruitlands was a Shaker* settlement, very well run by an efficient woman manager, in which all property was held in common and neither marriage nor family life was recognised. Lane and Bronson were much attracted by these people and, influenced by their doctrine, Lane declared that celibacy was essential to all creative thought and tried to persuade Alcott to leave his wife and children. Ten-year-old Louisa writes in her diary: "Mr L. was in Boston and we were glad. In the evening father and mother and Anna and I had a long talk. I was very unhappy and we all cried. Anna and I cried in bed and I

---

* The Shakers were a religious sect so called from the ecstatic fervour of their devotions.

prayed God to keep us all together"; and again: "Father and Mr L. had a talk and father asked us if *we* saw any reason for us to separate. Mother wanted to, she is so tired." These children had exchanged security for freedom like so many of their modern descendants. In the strictly regulated English Victorian nurseries the children did not run deliciously wild, to be found in company with beggar children on doorsteps, but neither did they take part in adult emotional discussions on ways and means or whether the family should stay together. The roof over their heads may sometimes have been stifling but it was safe.

Finally Charles Lane took himself off and Bronson Alcott took *himself* to his bed, where he lay for days without speaking, leaving Abba and his small daughters to manage as they could. Things would have gone hard indeed had not Emerson come to the rescue and Abba inherited a small legacy from her father. The family returned to Concord and it was typical of Abba's modernity that she insisted on them travelling by the new railroad, an adventurous proceeding in 1845.

Then an extraordinary thing happened. In spite of the discord which Charles Lane had brought about, in spite of the dislike which the children had shown to him, in spite of her husband's quarrel with him and subsequent breakdown, Abba invited him back ostensibly as tutor to the girls. He came and Bronson Alcott immediately left home, but Charles remained under the same roof as Abba the whole of that summer only leaving in the autumn, whereupon her husband returned and all was apparently as before. What was the meaning of this strange episode in Abba's life? Why did she invite Lane to come? Was it to try and heal the quarrel? If so it was obvious from the start that this was hopeless. Was it to show her power over the two men or was there something between this apostle of celibacy and the philosopher's wife? What did the children think of it and why did the neighbours apparently swallow this curious state of affairs with neither remonstrance nor scandal? Nothing is clear except that such flouting of the conventions by a middle-class Victorian wife in England would have been utterly impossible without swift retribution.

After Bronson's return he tried to earn a little by lecturing and writing. On one occasion he had been on an exploratory lecturing tour and his arrival home was greeted by the youngest girl enquiring eagerly: "Well, did they pay you?' Bronson ruefully produced one dollar, all that was left in his purse. He explained that he had had many promises but no payments and had lost his cloak and been forced to buy another. There was a pause and then Abba remarked: "Well, I call that doing *very* well!" The tale is told by Louisa to illustrate her mother's wonderful spirit but surely "the lady did protest too much", even though she added, "Since you are safely home, dear, we don't ask any more." But the fact remained that she did ask more and was often unhappy and dissatisfied with her life. Louisa's diary records: "I can't talk to any one but mother about my troubles and she has so many now to bear I try not to add any more." Abba disliked Concord, for one thing, and was always hankering after Boston. One day a friend came in and finding her in tears said: "Come to Boston and I will find you employment."

The escape was rationalised as economic necessity, but in reality the financial situation was then less desperate than it had been, for the two elder girls had started early to earn a little by teaching and Bronson's lecturing prospects were slowly improving. But the interest and independence offered by a post as paid social worker in her beloved Boston was too tempting to put aside. She left the household to the care of Beth and threw herself with enthusiasm into her work where she produced excellent written reports though on the personal side she was not very successful, being too impatient and hot-tempered. After a time she set up a domestic agency which went well. Louisa, always stoutly idolising her mother, represents this as a heroic sacrifice and indeed Abba was not above representing it as such herself, but there is no doubt she enjoyed it. She removed the family temporarily to Boston but eventually bought a house at Concord and retired to it.

It had early been impressed upon Louisa that she was destined to become an authoress and the support of her mother in her old age. Abba's frustrated ambitions for her husband fastened upon her clever little daughter and this time they were amply fulfilled. Louisa became famous and affluent and Abba basked in the comforts heaped upon her: "Mother is to be cosey if money can do it. She seems to be now for she sits in a pleasant room with no work, no care, no poverty to worry."

Did Abba, exulting in the fulfilment of her dream, ever reproach herself for Louisa's frequent breakdowns and feverish spells of overwork? There is no evidence that the responsibility for this ever came home to her even though, ironically, Louisa found it impossible to live with the mother she adored. She had to take lodgings in Boston to be able to write. Ironically, too, the husband Abba had written off *did* become famous and honoured but only after her death.

There was something of the vampire about Abba Alcott (the shade of gentle Marmee March shivers at the thought). Yet she was in her way a forerunner, boldly unconventional, efficient at a professional job, holding the family together through many a crisis, and the story of her married life, with its democratic ideals, its insecurity, its dissatisfactions and reaching after change, seems to belong rather to the world of today than to the mid-nineteenth century.

Hannah Pearsall Smith
1832-1911

"I came gradually to think of her as one of the wickedest people I had ever known . . . she carried feminism to such length that she found it hard to keep her respect for the Deity, since he was male. In passing a public house she would remark: 'Thy housekeeping, O Lord! if the Creator had been female there would have been no such thing as alcohol.' She taught her family that men are brutes and fools but women are saints . . . Her treatment of her husband was humiliating in the highest degree. She never spoke to him or of him except in a tone that made her contempt obvious—no one capable of mercy could have done it."

This was Bertrand Russell's opinion of his mother-in-law, Hannah Pearsall Smith, given in the first volume of his autobiography.

Here are two other portraits of her, one by her son, the writer Logan Pearsall Smith, the other by her grand-daughter, Ray Strachey, both of them hard-hitting, unsentimental individuals:

"My beautiful straightforward Quaker mother, one of the kindest and best of mothers."

"Love to her meant really sharing the wishes of the person you loved as much when they went contrary to your own as when they agreed with them. At five years old I realised that some grown-up people are nice and some children, but this particular person was nicer than any."

"She brought us up to do nothing to make other people unhappy, to play no practical jokes for instance. The corners of her mouth were always turned up in a smile and even her wrinkles had a smiling turn at their ends."

Could it be that Bertrand Russell missed that smile? He had a brilliant intelligence and a fine wit but had he a reliable sense of humour? It is ironic that the atheist philosopher should be shocked at the Quaker preacher's attitude to the Deity, and that she who several times risked her reputation and even her livelihood by repudiating belief in Hell and refusing to preach anything but a God of Love should be pronounced incapable of mercy. And was it for a man, who, after many years of happy marriage, had calmly told his wife that he no longer loved her, to accuse anyone of marital cruelty? "I knew that she was still devoted to me and I had no wish to be unkind", Russell writes, but he deserted her all the same as he was to desert other devoted women. This treatment, however, he apparently felt bore no comparison to Hannah's treatment of her husband to whom, incidentally, she was loyal through many trials of his own making; to whom, though Russell may not have been aware of this, she addressed letters beginning "My own darling husband", and whom she describes in old age as sitting placidly with her, listening with indulgence to their grandchildren: "I cannot say that we agree with all they say but they are so good and right-minded that I do not feel any anxiety."

That Hannah recognised the undoubted fact that she was superior in intelligence, strength of character and integrity to her husband, that she felt that many women were sacrificed in marriage and believed that there were other careers in which they might have found a happier fulfilment—these opinions, if reversed, if held by a man about his wife and about men in general in relation to marriage, would have caused neither surprise nor horror, but in a woman they called forth such condemnation from even so rational a male as Bertrand Russell as to constitute wickedness.

Hannah Whitall, known as a religious writer under the initials "H.W.S.", was born in 1832 of Quaker stock in Philadelphia and married Robert Pearsall Smith, who was also a Friend, when she was nineteen. She was certainly always a feminist. Her niece, Carey, was one of the first women to graduate at Cornell University and then went on her own to study in Germany and was passionately upheld in this then unheard-of course by her aunt. Her elder daughter, Mary (who later married the famous art critic, Bernard Berenson), also decided on a college career. "Girls have a *right* to a College education", wrote her mother, "they ought to be made to get it, even if it had to be done at the point of the bayonet. But since the world is not yet sufficiently advanced for that, the least parents can do is to open the door very wide to every girl who feels the least desire for it herself."

From the outset of their joint career as religious teachers and preachers, Hannah was the equal of her husband in reputation. Their success both in England and America was enormous. Then, like Henry Ward Beecher, Robert, in middle age, managed to compromise himself with a female disciple with disastrous effects. The scandal had a twofold consequence. It put an end to their public ministry and it also undermined his personal belief. Without either religious conviction nor the self-confident fulfilment hitherto provided by his career as a popular preacher, his flamboyant and histrionic personality was sadly diminished and he retired into the background of family life.

Not so Hannah. No scandal attached to her, her firm and sincere faith continued to flourish, though in her own words she grew "Broad, Broader, Broadest" and her "orthodoxy fled to the winds". She gave up preaching but she often spoke from temperance and pacifist platforms, worked hard for women's causes and continued to advise her many devoted followers on both sides of the Atlantic. Her most popular book was her first, *The Christian's Secret of a Happy Life*, and her attitudes towards this tremendously best seller was typical:

> "I must repeat that I *did* write 'The Christian's Secret' at the point of the bayonet, as it were. I did not want to write it at all, and only did it at Father's earnest entreaties. He had started a paper, which I thought was a great mistake, and I declared I would not write a line for it. But he begged so hard that at least I said I would write one article and no more, if he would give up drinking wine at dinner. Then when that article was published everybody clamoured for another, and Father begged and I was good-natured and went on, but under a continual protest. And the best chapter of all was written on a voyage over from America to England, when I was sea-sick all the time and as near cursing as a person who had experienced the "blessing of holiness" could dare to be! So tell BB [Bernard Berenson] books can be succesful even if they *are* ground out with groans and curses, and I feel very hopeful of his book. The great point is to have something to say, and this he has."

But all her public work was never allowed to infringe on the needs of her family. Ray Strachey wrote: "We, as children, had not the faintest notion that she was a religious teacher. She never preached to us but just took it for granted that we should be good." Young creatures could always rely on her for sympathy and indulgence, from the days when she endured the discomforts and hazards of camping among the Rockies to please her own children and their friends to the time when she climbed to the top of a haystack at the bidding of her grandchildren. Once, when she was seriously ill, she said calmly to Mary who was nursing her: "Daughter, if I die, remember I've put the children's fireworks on the top shelf."

Her attitude to death was that of a truly believing Christian and very rare. Though the loss of a little five-year-old daughter, of another at eleven and of her eldest son at eighteen were terrible blows, she yet could write: "I never did care very much how I fared myself if only my children were happy; and why should I care now, when a lot so much more blessed than anything my tenderest love could have compassed has been bestowed on them." And though no one could give a more vivid impression of wide interests and unbounded vitality Hannah welcomed each birthday as another milestone passed on the road to Heaven.

At fifty-four she exclaimed: "I confess I love graveyards that are such an unanswerable proof that we *shall* get rid of these old cocoons sometime, the sight of them always gives me a thrill of delight." Ten years later: "I had a prophecy from a 'palmist' the other day that I am to die at 67. Of course I place no faith in it, but I cannot say what a real inward spring of joy it gives me every now and then to think—'Suppose it should be true!'" And when she reached the seventies and was crippled with rheumatism she wrote to her daughter: "My sprees are really over at last. My next spree will be Heaven, and that *will* be a spree worth having!"

Hannah, who, according to Russell, taught her family that men are brutes and fools, was devoted to both her sons and had many men friends, including William James and George Macdonald. But it is true that her sympathies were most deeply aroused by women, many of whom came to her with their troubles: "My heart just aches for the misery, pure unmitigated misery, there is in this world . . . the other day I looked at a row [of women] and every one of them I knew, though no one else did, had husbands who made their lives one long torture"; "I have attended 2 meetings of Josephine Butler's on the subject of the infliction by England of the hor-

rible C.D. Acts upon the women of the nations they conquer
. . . My very soul blazed with indignation as I listened . . . I
cannot think that those old nations . . . who were doomed to
destruction because of their sins, *could* have been worse than
England!" But she continued to live there none the less.. She
and Robert had left America finally in 1888, chiefly because
their three remaining children had developed ties with England and they wished to be near them.

In a lighter vein she often showed her bias towards feminism. She rebukes her daughter for husband-hunting on behalf
of the beloved Ray: "It seems impossible that thee could have
wanted her to be caught at this early age." She did rather sadly
hold that the ideal marriage was seldom attainable. "I should
be only too delighted", she wrote to that same daughter, "if
I could believe thee really did adore BB. It is such a rare trait
in a wife that I could hardly believe it, but if it is true, thee
could not have a more secure foundation for happiness."

What she distrusted, and with reason, was marriage undertaken by a woman in default of any other possible way of life,
by young unthinking creatures who, if they were women, might
suffer all their lives as second-class citizens from the pressures
of society. Her son, Logan, tells this story of her when

> "she was full of years and famous for her religious teach-
> ings. A party of schoolgirls from some pious school in
> Philadelphia visited her 'as a venerable Quaker Saint' to
> hear from her own lips a few pious words. The spectacle
> of all these good young girls being prepared, as my mother
> knew, for lives of self-sacrifice as daughters or as wives—
> somehow this spectacle banished from the old lady's mind
> the admonition she had intended for them and when she
> opened her lips I was considerably surprised to hear her
> say, 'Girls, don't be too unselfish.'
>
> " 'Surely, mother,' I remonstrated with her afterwards,
> 'when those girls go home their pious relations will be
> dreadfully shocked at what thee said.'

" 'Yes,' she replied gaily, 'yes, I dare say it will make them grind their teeth.' "

If Hannah Pearsall Smith had been alive today she would certainly have sympathised with the Women's Liberation Movement, although she disliked and mistrusted any form of fanaticism. It was said of her that she liked men but she did not like husbands—in other words she disliked heartily the bondage to which she often saw women reduced by the state of marriage as it existed in the nineteenth century, and she had the hardihood to pronounce that there should be other ways in which a woman might fulfil herself.

Postscript

In 1846 a Mrs Ellis published a book entitled *Domestic Habits of the Women of England*. It became a bestseller. A sort of popular pious Victorian marriage guidance manual, it was full of sensible advice on the training of girls for their work in life as wives and mothers. The author is clearly not a conventional or rigid woman. She includes sound criticism of the fashionable cult of feminine helplessness and ignorance and of the unhealthy emptiness of many women's lives. This makes her unquestioning acceptance of their dependent and subservient position all the more telling:

> "In her intercourse with man, it is impossible but that woman should feel her own inferiority, and it is right that it should be so . . . she does not meet him on equal terms. Her part is to make sacrifices in order that his enjoyment may be enhanced. She does this with a willing spirit but she does it so often without grateful acknowledgment. Nor is man to be blamed for this."

Mrs Ellis explains that he is not to be expected to understand or even to know how she feels. Her part is to continue cheerfully to make these sacrifices without question and never to put her own needs or interests first, and this is to apply to brothers and fathers and sons as well as husbands:

> "If all was confusion and neglect at home—filial appeals unanswered, domestic comforts uncalculated, husbands, sons and brothers referred to servants for all the

little offices of social kindness, in order that the ladies of the family might hurry away to some committee room, scientific lecture, or public assembly, however laudable the object for which they met, there would be sufficient cause why their cheeks should be mantled with the blush of burning shame."

Most of the book is concerned with the apprenticeship for marriage. Once the vows have been pledged only the more practical and public observances are dealt with : the perpetually cheerful welcoming face, the ever neat parlour, the tastefully served meal, the ready self-effacing sympathy :

'Tis never women's part
Out of her fond misgivings to perplex
The fortune of the man to whom she cleaves.*

Any more intimate aspects of the married state were

"a theme too delicate for the handling of an ordinary pen and a venturing beyond that veil, which the sacredness of such a connection is calculated to draw over all that is extreme in the happiness or misery of human life."

Another reason she gives from sheering off any advice upon particular behaviour is that the "habits and temperaments" of the husband should in each case be taken into account. The habits and temperament of the wife, of course, do not matter— they must, whatever they may be, adapt themselves as best they can.

The maxims set forth in this book remained more or less unchallenged until the close of the century and are accepted by all the great mid-Victorian novelists, though the women among these, as we have seen, pondered upon them wistfully.

In her strictures upon the helplessness and ignorance of women, Mrs Ellis however found herself in a quandary for she

* Talfourd.

was forced to admit that men seemed to prefer them like that and men must have what they want. She was quick to find a praiseworthy excuse for them:

> "There is a peculiarity in men—I would fain call it benevolence, which induces them to offer the benefit of their protection to the most helpless and dependent of the female sex."

It does not seem even to have occurred to her that behind this chivalrous motive there might be the well-founded conviction that it is easier to maintain mastery over the weak than the strong.

Yet it was obvious to Mrs Ellis that this helplessness was bad for the wife's character and still more important, that it might sometimes prove inconvenient for the husband. How was she to manage then? She must become capable and healthy and hope that no one would notice. This often seemed to work. There was Thomas Carlyle, for instance, who was able to expatiate on the rightly dependent nature of women while he left a great deal of tiresome and exacting decisions and actions to his "essentially passive" little goody. So although the ivy must cling to the tower with its beautiful, soft and yielding foliage because the tower liked it so, it was better if it did not become *really* a parasite—a difficult and dangerous role to attempt.

Frances Power Cobbe, writing in 1868, declared that "the ideal the majority of men have formed of wedlock is the poetical vision . . . that a woman's whole life and being, her soul, body, time, property, thought and care ought to be given to her husband and that nothing short of such absorption in him and his interests makes her a true wife."

These were the two powerful concepts which formed the Victorian image of the married state: the clinging dependent ivy and the willing and capable slave. But the wind of change began to blow and it blew predominantly from the West. The idea of a woman's separate and equal identity had developed

207

more rapidly in the New World. We can see this in Caroline Norton's satiric echoes from the London clubs. Her clubmen are made to exclaim on the question of women's rights and wrongs: "Pooh, Pooh, nonsense, Bloomerism, Americanism! We can't have that sort of thing in England!" We can see it in the contrasts drawn between the women of the two nations by many writers of fiction and in the characters and destinies of actual lives.

As time went on, contacts between the old and new worlds became more frequent and more fruitful. Simultaneously, hard-won improvements in women's education and in their legal position began to break down the old stereotypes.

By the end of the century the helpless little wife grew to a normal size and pushed aside her sofa, the angels in the house folded up their wings, Mrs Benson discovered an identity, the ivy was pulled off the tower as a definitely unhealthy growth and the tower itself gradually assumed more domestic and sensible proportions.

Index